THE ANAM GLYPHS

A Universal Oracle for the Wise Seeker

BEAUTIMUS POTAMUS AND
PEGGY A. WHEELER

Copyright © 2018 Peggy A. Wheeler

All rights reserved. Reproduction or utilization of this work in any form, by any means now known or hereinafter invented, including, but not limited to, xerography, photocopying and recording, and in any known storage and retrieval system, is forbidden without permission from the copyright holder.

ISBN 978-1-988256-97-9

www.dragonmoonpress.com

Want to have your own deck of Anam Glyph Cards?

Order them here:

https://bit.ly/2OgvB2v

Dedicated to Steven D. Wheeler,
my life's partner, my best friend, my everything.
Without you
I would not plant gardens,
make oracles,
or co-write books with talking hippos.
Peggy A. Wheeler

Acknowledgments

For their support, guidance, friendship and inspiration, I am filled with gratitude for so many people that I cannot name them all. Here are but a few of the special people in my life I wish to acknowledge for their support of *The Anam Glyph* project.

Thank you, Denise Dumars, my long time friend, my former literary agent, and a superb author. As my friend, and former agent, you have been always supportive.

Thank you to my dear heart-space sister-friend, "Sue Bee" Bateman, who supported this effort from the get-go, and nagged me mercilessly until I submitted my manuscript and proposal to Denise way back in the day.

A huge hug and many thanks go to my daughter, Aimee, and to my granddaughters, Brittany Ross and Gianna Marie, my muses. You three inspire me.

Much gratitude to my writing partners, Christine Stabile, and Will Weisser who kept me and my story on track. And a huge thanks you to my publisher, Gwen Gades, of Dragon Moon Press.

Most of all, I am grateful to my husband, critic, partner, and very best friend who puts up with a lot from me, always with grace, class, and humor. I love you with my entire being, my dearest, Steve.

Contents

Now, We Begin!	19
How to Cast Your Glyphs	33
Consulting the Anam Glyphs	40
Alma	41
Angelwing	44
Cúpla	47
Cynn	51
Djinn	54
Dream Lizard	57
Feoh Cup	59
Greenleaf	62
Hearthand	65
Maahe	68
Moonmajick	71
Motherbelly	74
Openeye	77
Pelé Fire	79
Pleiadian Key	83
Ram	88
Rest Time	91
Royal Elk	95
Sacred Trio	98
Seagull	101
Self Love	103
Sequoia	106
Spirit Bridge	109
Stone Wheel	115
Tricky Boy	119
Twentynine	123
Waterbug	126

Waterfall	128
Wheatharvest	130
White Light	133
Yorushi	136
Zephyr	140
To Conclude Our Time Together	144

A Note from Peggy A. Wheeler, Lady Beautimus' Co-Author

That night I'd been drinking wine. That's true of every night, but a few hours earlier I'd lost my third job in seven months, so in an effort to self-medicate I had consumed more than usual. As a result, I went all slushy and soggy. Translation: I'd achieved a state I refer to as "Tipsy Woozie."

I had poured another glass of the red when out of the big blue ether, a noisy otherworldly crackling, buzzing and popping filled my apartment. The smell of sulfur flooded my nostrils, and triggered a coughing fit so profound I thought I might lose a lung. For a moment I thought a hell demon may have come to drag me to the netherworld. I picked up my phone and prepared to dial Emergency, thinking if not a demon, then a terrible and murderous electrical fire had broken out in my apartment walls, and I might be fried alive.

As abruptly as the sound and stink came to me, the noise ceased, and the odor dissipated. After a thorough room inspection revealed no fire or smoke, and I found no trace of demons, I settled back in to my easy chair, wine in one hand, and book in another. "Must have been something outside, maybe some sort of traffic noise. It's gone now. What do you think, Peaches?" My calico rubbed against my legs, her purr like a helicopter. I had resumed reading "One Hundred Years of Solitude," by Gabriel Garcia Marquez when the lights dimmed as if by magic, and a grainy image of a full-sized female purple-eyed hippopotamus appeared on my living room wall. I dropped my book with a splat against the hardwood floor and spilled precious wine all over my pajamas, the only good pair I owned. I don't know what upset me more, the waste of good pinot noir, my ruined jammies, or the hallucination.

The image resembled an old-time movie, not unlike the 8mm films Grandma used to take of us kids when we were toddlers, only this hippo appeared in life-like color, rather than sepia or that particular black-and-white of the time. "No, can't be." I clenched my eyes shut, and reopened them. The image remained steadfast. But when I looked over my shoulder I saw no one else in the room, and certainly no projector anywhere. I dismissed the hippo as a Tipsy Woozie vision.

I prepared to dump the last of my bottle of wine, swear off the grape forever, and then stand under a blistering hot shower until sober. But as I began my retreat to the bathroom, the hippo spoke to me in clear, articulate English, "Hello? Can you see me? This is Beautimus Potamus, and I need to ask a favor of you, Peggy." That's when I stumbled and nearly fell backwards over Peaches, who demonstrated her displeasure by grabbing my left calve with both set of forepaws and digging in her claws until blood ran down to my ankle.

Beautimus Potamus from the green planet, Rendaz, had called to ask me to be her Subject Matter Expert in all things Earthean for her book, The Anam Glyphs. I had no idea at that time I would also be her co-author, and in my craziest Tipsy Woozie moments, I could have never imagine that I'd become friends with a talking hippo on a distant planet.

"Why, me?" I asked her.

"Because I like your spirit. I've been observing you for years through my Crystal Interface."

"You have?" I didn't ask what a Crystal Interface might be.

"Yes, indeed. I need someone like you to help me verify information, and act as my Hu Man guide through the mysterious and often confounding culture of your planet. Of the thousands of possibilities, and after observing your growth from bubbit to adult, I chose you."

I closed my eyes again, and reopened them. Yup, still there. "You're not real. I've had too much to drink, I'm upset over losing my job, I'm tired, I spilled my wine and ruined my jammies. To top it off, my cat scratched me. I'm bleeding all over the place, and it's likely to get infected, dammit. I know for a fact you can't be talking to me. This is not possible."

The hippo rocked side-to-side in what I could only interpret as a gesture of frustration. "Is that what you honestly believe?"

"Please go away right now. You're scaring me."

"Oh my. I didn't mind to frighten you. I'd only hoped you'd be open to helping me. I suppose I will have to find another writer to…"

"I'm not a writer! I'm not an expert on Earth culture or history. I'm not anything but an unemployed office worker who can't hold down a simple job, and now I think I may be going crazy talking with a hippo projected on my living room wall. Why me?"

"I told you, I like your spirit, and you are most assuredly a writer. You simply don't know it, yet."

I have experienced some bizarre, surrealistic events through the years, so I was open—a little, at least—to the notion there is much in our universe we cannot yet explain. Besides that, this hippo seemed kindly enough. "I'll tell you what, Beautimus. I'm going to shower, swallow an aspirin, go to bed and sleep this off. If you're the real deal, come back tomorrow night, and we'll talk." At that, with a pop and a flash of greenish light, the image vanished.

The following night, instead of wine, I drank peppermint tea to keep my wits about me on the off-off-off-chance the hippo from outer space might return. I had downed the last of my tea before I gave up waiting. "Well, that's it. Just as I thought, there are no talking hippos from other planets visiting you, old girl. You have to stop drinking."

I put my empty tea cup and saucer on the coffee table, and headed to bed with Peaches trotting close behind. I'd not taken four steps before the otherworldly crackling, buzzing, and popping filled the room, and the sulfur fumes assaulted me once again. I nearly tripped over Peaches, who let out a yowl and streaked off to hide under the bed. I turned, and there, on the blank wall, in all her big beautiful hippo glory, the image of Beautimus Potamus appeared, staring at me with those purple eyes. "Well, how about it? Will you help me?"

A Note to Hu Mans from Beautimus Potamus

Welcome wise seeker! I am Beautimus Potamus from the planet Rendaz. I am Professor of Earthly Things at Dr. Pimbly's School of Goodly Educated Adults, a writer, and a lover of the supreme Great Goddess Genesis.

My planet is an emerald green globe, double the size of Earth, located in the far outlying reaches beyond Arcturus. We've two moons, Lady Luz and Lady Beth, and two suns, Purmoso and Racine. Rendaz has one massive ocean full of fish and water beasts, and our volcanic lands are crossed, dotted, and splashed by rivers, ponds, pools, waterfalls, and streams, all with the most loquacious fish you will ever encounter. The trout tribe, especially, are a chatty group.

All manner of mammals, reptiles, arachnids, and insects live on Rendaz. Many, such as dinosaurs, Sasquatch, and Jackalopes are now extinct on your blue planet, Earth. And, all of us save those born mute, talk. We work. We attend school. We raise families. We live, laugh and play much like Hu Mans, and we are beset by many of the same frailties that citizens of the blue planet suffer from. There are murderers and thieves among us on Rendaz, and we fall in love and get our hearts broken. Some of us struggle with jealousies, low self-esteem, frustrations, excess liver heat, and depression. But compared to Earthians, we are peaceful. We live and work together cooperatively, the ant tribes side-by-side with the T-Rex tribes, the Praying Mantis tribe next to the Hippo tribe. As a matter of fact, my best friend on Rendaz is Samuel S. Goodwings, a lime green praying mantis. He generally rides on my head as we walk and discuss scholarly matters, and we attend all the festivals together.

You Hu Mans are too violent and unpredictable, so none of you are allowed on our planet. It's highly unlikely that any

Rendazian would intentionally communicate with any Hu Man, but there are exceptions—My need to procure Hu Man assistance with the writing of this book being one. I had to seek out a Hu Man to help me better understand the ups and downs and sideways of Earthly existence, and, also, because so many of the symbols for The Anam Glyphs come from Earth.

I first observed Peggy A. on my Crystal Interface when she was but a mere bubbit. I watched her grow and develop over time, and eventually, I noticed similarities between us. As examples, she likes strawberries, as do I. She has been plagued by self-doubt and low self-esteem, as I have been. She likes dogs. I like dogs, especially my friend, Buford, who sometimes joins me on my morning walks. Although Buford is ill-educated, and tends to slobber, we do enjoy lovely chats. And, Peggy A. writes stories, as do I.

Of course, Hu Mans do not have the sensibilities of hippos. I had to work with Peggy A. closely to help her develop enough "hippo sense" so we could work together. Although an apt and eager student, she's not quite there yet. I'm afraid you Hu Mans can be a little slow, but I have hopes for her because she's proven herself to be at the very least somewhat teachable. I was delighted when she finally demonstrated enough sense to assist me with this project.

Her job is to add Earthian knowledge to the interpretations of the symbols, and to use her Hu Man hands and opposable thumbs to enter the information into her Earth computer, so I can transfer the information onto my Crystal Interface. She has done an adequate job, for which I am most grateful. I now consider Peggy A. my friend, as well. We talk about our love lives, and our bubbits. She and I both have daughters, now grown. We discuss our jobs. After a time of unemployment, she's at last secured a position as a Technical Writer. Not bad for a woman whose prior experience was limited to entering things into a primitive keyboard where one has to actually press little buttons to make words and figures appear on paper or screen, and talking to people who call on the TeleFone.

One other thing we've in common is the show "I Love Lucy." Peggy A. watched reruns on her TeleVision Set growing up. I still stream the show on my Crystal Interface. That episode where Lucy and Ethel worked on the chocolate assembly line is my absolute favorite. But, we cannot get too close, Peggy A. and I. Her lifespan is but a fraction of mine, and if I allow myself to become too attached, the grief of her passing may be too difficult for me to bear with grace. I, therefore, keep her at muzzle's length.

As an aside, do you Hu Mans know we contacted your scientists in the lands known as Russia and America when you instigated your primitive space program? We thought to help. We even contacted your people at NASA to offer assistance. To our surprise, instead of accepting our help, every single one of the men in white shirts and thin pieces of cloth around their necks called "ties" dissolved into a an absolute tizzy. I assume you've heard the expressions, "Huston, we have a problem," or "Danger! Danger! Will Robinson"? Those phrases were first uttered before you even put a little helpless monkey in a rocket capsule, and shot him off into space where you left him to die. Or, was that a dog? No matter. Either way, barbaric! But, I digress. We Rendazians were rather insulted when your Earthian scientists and leaders chose to hide our communications and interactions from the rest of your world. Because of that concealment most Hu Mans have no idea we exist. I did read several articles in your *National Enquirer*, the only source of factual media on your planet, there are Hu Mans who have interacted in recent history with our ships and our people. Therefore, our presence is known to some of you, at least.

Peggy A. Wheeler knows about us, of course, but when I asked if she might spread the word, her response? "If I told anyone I knew a talking hippo from another planet that projects her image on my living room wall, and we are writing a book together, I'd be carted off for a psych evaluation."

I thought it over, and came to realize her assumption is entirely logical and reasonable, because if Rendazians knew I had formed a relationship with an actual Hu Man, and engaged her as my subject matter expert for the writing of my book, The Anam Glyphs, they, too, would be skeptical. My friends, colleagues at Dr. Pimbly's, and family may question my judgment, if not my sanity. I dare not tell Samuel S. Goodwings because he'd mock me for eons.

I did tell my good friend, Lizzy, a mastodon I've known since childhood, and with whom I studied ballet at Auntie Nancie's School of Fancy Dancing. Although I consider Sam my best friend, Lizzy is a close second, and the one I talk to about womanly things, and writerly things. I know she'd never judge me for working with a Hu Man. I also told my spiritual teacher, Lady Rhianna, a 300-year-old blue crane. She clicked her beak and flapped her wings in joy. "Oh, this is marvelous. A Rendazian and a Hu Man working together. Imagine that!"

Both women cautioned me, however, to keep my relationship with the Earthly beings close to my hide, otherwise, too many Randazians would not understand. The males, especially, might think me irrational, and that won't do for a professor.

What you don't know, at least I can't see anything about it in any of your Earthian history books, is that we on Rendaz discovered your planet when nothing of merit existed on Earth. We gave you language, art, science, and taught you rudimentary manners. We also brought Rendazians to help populate your planet. That is why you've horses, rabbits, elephants, birds, and such. There were no Rendazians when we touched down in our first Arc, so mating couples two-by-two volunteered to remain on Earth to be of service, and to ensure your survival. On our second mission we brought many fruiting plants and trees.

When we encountered your species, you could not speak, ate only grubs, roots, and wild grass shoots, with the exception in the Americas where blue corn and cranberries grew. This scarcity of food variety proved inadequate nutrition to sustain a growing population of living beings, though, which explains why there were so few of you back then. We traveled many times in those early days to your planet to help the new species we named Hu Man, which in old Rendazian means "New Man."

Once we taught you language, we all got along famously. Then the meteor hit, and most of you Hu Mans, and the Rendazians among you, perished. Other Rendazians, such as dinosaurs and Jackalopes, disappeared completely. Enough survived this extinction event to rebuild, but things between Rendazians and Hu Mans were never the same.

To complicate matters further, the meteor brought with it a terrible virus which affected only Rendazians. The meteor spread its poison through the atmosphere and rendered all Rendazians on Earth mute, with the exception of some parrots and a few dogs. Over time, Hu Mans reduced Rendazians from allies and teachers, to slaves, mere pets, and even food. Awful, I tell you, awful. Your history is sullied by the violence done to the very Rendazians who had taught you civilized ways, helped you to survive, and otherwise gave you everything you needed to live better lives.

There are Rendazians who believe we should send deadly stink bombs to destroy all Hu Mans, but after decades of heated deliberation, The Butterfly Council and the Old Trees passed laws forbidding us to harm any sentient beings on other planets, and that's the only reason any of you are still on Earth.

I, personally, am fascinated by Hu Mans, and began several hundreds of years ago to study your culture. Your musicians, poets, and philosophers are indeed a treasure, and worth preserving.

It was through my studies I discovered Earthian archetypal symbols that have within them great meaning in many of your countries, and thus began my painstaking work of cataloging them. What I discovered, as I mentioned, is that we, meaning Hu Mans and Rendazians, are much the same in surprising ways. We are all made of the same "star stuff," as some of your philosophers and spiritual folks say. We are interconnected, all related, Hu Man and Rendazian, but over many thousands of years, we have disconnected.

My Aunt Meg and Uncle Phalen who, unlike me, are non-believers think my work with the Anam Glyphs is utter claptrap. "Oh, Bea," my aunt says, "You'd be better served to leave this hooey alone, and concentrate on teaching your Earthean History classes."

"No, Auntie, I say to her. "I know in my heart of hearts, writing this book is part of my life's purpose, and I hope one day this work, and the Glyphs, will bring Hu Mans and Rendazians back into alignment with one another."

"Suit yourself, dear," Uncle Phalen says, "but, I can tell you with certainty that Rendazians will never reunite with Hu Mans."

"We shall see! Shan't we?" I so wanted to say that aloud, but out of respect for my aunt and uncle, who raised me after my mother passed away and my father abandoned me, I kept that last bit locked tight in my head. Lady Rhianna always says, "Because you think something does not mean it's wise to let it drop out of your maw."

The Anam Glyphs

I believe the Anam Glyphs are one set of tools we can use to discover the means to reconnect. Once every being comes to know without doubt that we are the same we can work together for the advancement of Hu Mans and Rendazians alike. That is why, in working with the Anam Glyphs, you may notice the theme of connectedness threading its way through some of the interpretations and descriptions.

Over the last several hundreds of years, I have worked with oracles from many different traditions, but I've always been most drawn to what I call "stones and bones," primitive divination tools made of natural materials such as rock, wood, bone, or clay. In the Earth decades of the 1980s, my first experience working with stone oracles occurred when I happened to stream Ralph Blum's *The Book of Runes* on my Crystal Interface. With the help of my house squirrels, I crafted my own set of Viking Runes, and used them so often that I wore out my first set. I made another. I own Rune sets inscribed on colored polished gemstones. I have a set made from *Ohlo De Boi* ("Eye of the Bull" in your Portuguese language) a magical seed said to bring prosperity to the owner, and I have made Rune sets fashioned from the red clay of The River Kwa near my abode, and from color shifting Shar Stones from our Oceanic District.

I did not set out initially to create my own "stones and bones" oracle. The Anam Glyphs sort of *happened* to me. However, the first thing I noticed about them is their symbols emerged from both Rendazian and Earth traditions and mythology rather than from a single originating culture or convention. These stones (which of course, work nicely as cards, too) honor everyone, and are for everyone, no matter their ethnicity, heritage, species, spiritual practice or belief system. Since the Glyphs are not Rendazian, or Earthian, they are "universal stones," and since I believe the Glyphs were given to me as a gift from the Goddess, or the universal "soul place" which connects us all, I felt it important to acknowledge and honor this precious gift by recognizing its origins. This is why I named this collection of symbols "anam" meaning "soul" or "spirit" in your Irish Gaelic language.

My greatest hope is the Glyphs provide you with answers to your most pressing life's questions, and assist you in manifesting your desires. Above all, I wish for you to have a lot of fun with them. Oh, and by the way, when writing the interpretation for Tricky Boy, for mysterious reasons, the formatting completely went haywire. I'm proficient in the many word processing programs on the Crystal Interlace, and my Hu Man writing partner, Peggy A. Wheeler, has been working with Word Tables for years, which is how we created our initial drafts of the symbols themselves. We worked together to do everything we knew to correct the formatting. The harder we tried to make the corrections, the more our efforts made matters worse. When you read the interpretation under Tricky Boy, I hope you laugh as hard as my writing partner and I did! Tricky Boy is my personal favorite because he teaches me the most about myself. So it is.

May the Goddess hold you and keep you in her hands.

How the Anam Glyphs Found Me

The first of the Glyphs emerged from a series of lucid dreams I experienced many moons ago. In my sleep, usually just before dawn, an image simply appeared to me suspended in mid-air. For the first eight of the thirty-two symbols, I asked my house squirrel, Applecheeks, to draw on a tablet I kept on my altar. Over time, I had covered the tablet with messages, receipts, and a motley assortment of paper scraps until the odds and ends of notes completely obscured the images. Then one day, my mother, Sangrina, who had long before passed into the arms of the Great Goddess Genesis, came to me in a vision. "Bea, you have to do something with those glyph symbols. Promise me."

By then, I had nearly forgotten all about them, and wasn't even sure where I'd put them. After lengthy and frantic searching, and with the help of both of my squirrel helpers, I eventually uncovered them. I have to give the most credit to Agnes. She and her sister, Applecheeks have been with me for undreds of years, and we've become quite close.

Born mute, Applecheeks lets Agnes do all the talking for them both. As if to make up for her sister's silence, Agnes talks and talks and talks, always in one breath, usually ending her run-on sentences with a question. But, beyond being a great talker, Agnes is a great "finder of things," so I was not in the least surprised when she announced, "Bea-I-thought-you-kept-those-glyphs-on-your-goddess-altar-I'll-look-there-if-I-find-them-I'll-bring-them-right-to-you-do-you-want-lilac-tea-this-morning-with-breakfast?" Yes, she had found them, and she and Apple dragged the tablet to me, and for the first time in a very long while I laid my eyes on the first eight symbols.

Soon after, I visited my friend, Calypso, a trout unfortunately afflicted with ADHD who lives in the River Kwa. As I bathed and she swam about me, we entered into a lively conversation about the Turkey Buzzards, who we'd read about in our periodical, The Daily Quacker. The buzzards were forever filing law suits for one reason or another, and had employed a Komodo Dragon attorney. That's another story for another time. But, the point is, sometimes in the most unexpected manner, we receive validation. Our conversation about buzzards turned into one of those validating moments.

"Calypso," I said. "I'm always on the side of the buzzards in these things, but sometimes I find myself annoyed with how litigious they can be. Even the slightest benign comment…"

"Oh, you mean the specieism thing they're unhappy about? I get that. We trout sometimes are discriminated against by the salmon tribe. They think they are so special with their pink flesh, and all and—ooooh, what's that?" She leapt from the water and came down with a noisy splash. "There's something in the river. Right there. See? Should we check it out, Bea? Now, were we talking about something?"

"Yes, we were talking about…"

"That's right, a Komodo Dragon!"

"No, we were talking about the buzzards who had hired the Komodo Dragon…oh, never mind."

"Buzzards? Oh yeah. I remember now. Bea! Look! There's something stuck in the fissure in that river rock there. I must swim over. Could be breakfast."

I followed her, and when I happened to look down into the water where Calypso circled the thing in the fissure, which turned out to be nothing but a strand of sticky pink river grass. But, to my surprise and delight, there in the river bottom I saw as clear as the morning light two symbols I had dreamed about. One of the symbols, Ram, appeared submerged barely beneath the water's surface on a boulder, as though someone had purposely drawn it there. Another, Mahee, rested on the sandy bottom of the river. The symbols in the water were only the beginning of a series of magical occurrences that afternoon.

Iridescent water bugs appeared to me everywhere on the creek's surface, gliding over the water effortlessly, in view then out of view, almost as though appearing and disappearing at will. I felt a great connection to these ephemeral water dancers, and I began to receive clear impressions from them. "Waterbug" was to assume an honored place among the Anam Glyphs.

Then on the sandy banks of the creek, lizards emerged from the low-lying Canji Brush, dozens and dozens of lizards. I witnessed one of them at the water's edge, a tiny juvenile hunting its prey, catching and consuming it. Only inches away from where I stood, this little green creature, completely at ease, took his nourishment in my presence, allowing me to view his part in the larger cycle of nature. I attached myself to the *Spirit of Lizard* and knew in that moment "Dream Lizard," too, would be included as part of the Anam Glyphs. I returned home to research the deeper meaning of the lizard. Many lizard myths exist within several cultures on Earth, but most all have a common root meaning. In conducting my research, time and time again I read that Lizard comes into our lives to tell us to pay close attention to our dreams.

In the weeks following my encounter with Calypso that day at the river, my dreaming of symbols returned. I dreamed of numbers, lines, colors, and shapes. Sometimes in my waking hours I mentally caught a flash of a specific image. The symbols came at me faster and faster, day, night, in the morning, during my sleeping hours, and in my waking hours.

Sometimes, I'd find myself in the drowsy minutes before dawn with a word in my maw. One early morning, I woke Agnes and Applecheeks because in my sleep I repeated aloud the word, "zephyr, zephyr, zephyr." Another time, for three nights in a row, I dreamed about the Earth number twenty-nine.

With the help of a lemur artist, I sketched all the symbols for the Glyphs, asked their names, and wrote about them, all the while pushing out of my mind any thought that what I documented might be right or wrong, accurate or inaccurate, complete or incomplete. At times, I grew inspired to further research a particular symbol to more fully add meaning to its description, but my initial process was always the same—study the symbol and write about it in a stream of consciousness until I felt complete.

When it grew apparent that many of the symbols originated on Earth rather than Rendaz, I began my search for a Hu Man to help me with my research, ergo, my relationship with Peggy A. Wheeler.

The Significance of the Anam Glyph Symbols

I'm fascinated by symbols, which is probably why I attracted the Anam Glyph images in the first place. Symbols can be more powerful than spoken words because they cross language barriers and generally have universal meaning connected to our "collective unconscious," as the Earth Hu Man, Jung says. Often, the meanings in symbols are so highly charged, or so complex, that mere words are inadequate to express their significance.

Our communal relationship to symbols is as ancient as the appearance of Rendazians on Rendaz, and Hu Mans on The Blue Planet. The first symbols appeared when Lilith, the Hebrew mythological predecessor to Eve who dwelled in a special garden on Earth, scratched a mark on a tree that meant something to her. There are many books available on the subject of signs and symbols. Pick one up and discover for yourself how meaningful symbols are in your life!

While conducting research, I read a wonderful interview on between Dr. Jim Euclid, a freelance writer living in Melbourne, Australia, and Reiki Master, Chiara Tina. In his interview with Master Chiara, which Dr. Euclid titled *Symbols and Signs*, he states…

Spiritual symbolism, where inner states are mirrored by outer events, is as old as humanity itself. Our mind uses physical objects (totems, icons and mantras) as means of representing our inner feelings and emotions… The more symbolic our daily life is, the more imbued it is with symbols, and the more symbols and signs begin to appear in our everyday life…and with them comes a responsibility of acting upon the advice given.

The Anam Glyphs contain meaning which transcends my interpretation. When I study the images on the Glyphs I wonder what else they might mean, what significance someone else may assign to them, or what actions some people may choose to take as a result of the Anam Glyph symbols which could result in a positive difference to them as sentient beings, and to both our planets. What do you perceive when you look at the symbols on the Glyphs? Where have you seen these marks before?

From Whence These Symbols Hail

None of the symbols on the Glyphs are original, meaning I take no credit for them because I did not create or invent them. My years of research revealed some originate from Earth in prehistoric cave drawings, or from your indigenous peoples' pantheon of symbols. Some come from the Hebrew language, others from the Nordic Runes, some from sacred Hindu text, others from Buddhism, some from the Christian tradition, others from the Wiccan tradition. They come from Australian aboriginal myth, from African spirituality, and from ancient Goddess legends throughout the universe. Some were given to me from nature, others from popular sources such as those I sparked to in magazines or movies I streamed on my Crystal Interface, and others appeared from, well, who knows where!

One symbol felt so familiar it was like an old friend. It kept calling to me. At a goddess gathering, as I engaged in a discussion with a Hoary Puffleg about a particular glyph, it occurred to me that it came from the original Star Trek television series that I'd viewed on my Crystal Interface decades before! Peggy A. and I got a good laugh out of that one. For reasons unknown to me, these archetypes kept appearing to me, one after another.

What This Guide on the Glyphs Include

- Description
- Origin
- Interpretation
- (Optional) Exercise

The Glyphs and their meanings are based solely on Peggy A. Wheeler's, and my own consciousness, intuitive sense and understanding. Resting in the pillows on the floor of my abode adjacent to my Interface, I became still and allowed all impressions to flow from my heart and mind to the Interface screen without censorship. I can't say the symbols "spoke to me" as much as they generated some sort of energy I "sensed" as true. "I feel that as well," Peggy A. told me. As we worked together, at times, what Peggy A. thought and felt about the Glyphs materialized on my Interface screen as though she'd willed it. Our minds and hearts vibrating in tune caused her thoughts to appear in words as if by magic.

If you resonate with our interpretations, and they are meaningful to you, that is wonderful. If your sense or understanding is different from ours, or you do not resonate with them the same way Peggy A. and I do, that's wonderful, too. If you are moved to do so, we encourage you to apply your own creative wisdom and knowledge to the symbols on the Anam Glyphs and respond to them accordingly.

Exercises

The optional exercise helps you more easily overcome obstacles, to achieve a specific goal, to focus and reinforce the "intention" of the Glyph, or to better connect with the great Goddess, or your internal light, the core of your sacred being.

My spiritual mentor, Lady Rhianna—I mentioned her earlier, you may recall—is the high priestess of the Wayflower District where I live. Or, did I mention that already? May have. At over 200-years old myself, and with all these crazy middle-age hot flashes, I get a little forgetful. Anyway, she told me the exercises are necessary. "Bea, the idea of exercises is that with the *doing* comes more easily the *manifestation*. Reading the Glyphs will not, in themselves, create significant change. There must also be action in direct line with the messages, or not much happens."

I suggest you perform some of the exercises and see if blessings materialize, and answers to big questions come to you with more ease and speed than had you not.

Power Stones

There are five of these in the Anam Glyphs. If in a reading, a Power Stone appears, its message has deep relevance to your other Glyphs. This Glyph tells you your current issue is directly in line with your life's progress. When a Power Stone lands in your layout in the Destiny position, pay particular attention. Its message could be life-altering.

The "Ancient" Anam Glyph Altar

You may wonder how there can be an ancient Anam Glyph altar when the Anam Glyphs are new. First of all, the symbols on the Glyphs are not new. They may be as old as Hu Mans and Rendazians themselves. And altars are "older than old."

A Short History of Altars

Those of you experienced Wiccan or other pagan practitioners, or who are Hindu or Buddhist, or worship the Goddess as do I, or are priests and priestess of your many faiths, are familiar with the concept of creating a sacred space.

There is hardly a religion on Earth that doesn't use an altar. Altars figure prominently in Wiccan ceremonies, in Christian Churches, and Shinto Temples. You'll find altars in the Taoist, indigenous, Norse, Celtic and African pagan conventions. Ancient Mayan, Aztec, Greek, Roman, and Egyptians worshiped and performed ceremonies at altars. Anthropologists have discovered altars on Earth and Rendaz that are many thousands of years old. On Rendaz, there is but one religion, and it is centered on Great Goddess Genesis and her lesser goddesses. If you are a believer, as am I, you will have an altar in your abode.

The purpose of an altar is to connect with the divine to ask for a blessing, to give thanks, set an intention, or honor a deity or ancestor. An altar makes tangible the intangible, and creates a physical sacred space for us to more easily focus on our daily prayer, or meditation.

Part of the purpose in the Anam Glyphs is to help us to better recognize and more clearly define our desires. Each Glyph has within it an overt or implied intention for you, which you can, with very little practice, easily uncover. For example, if you pull *Greenleaf*, the intention is you will either be healed, or will become a healer.

The overt intention in *Feoh Cup is for you to attract Earth money, or Rendazian Glow Seeds, while Cynn* implies an intention for you to foster better family relationships, or attract people who will become non-biological family. When you discover your "intent" within the Glyph, keeping your stones on your altar will infuse your intention with power because it then becomes a part of your conscious sacred focus.

If you already have an altar, your work is nearly done. All you need do is designate a special place on your altar to hold your Anam Glyphs.

I made an altar from clay in the shape of a faceless Hu Man goddess. I named my goddess Prosperia, and mounted her on a base with spaces to hold an incense stick, a few small candles, a crystal and small offerings such as rice, salt, wine, bits of cake, or a fresh flower. I pull three glyphs each day. I ask one of my house squirrels to place them on my Prosperia altar, light a candle, and ignite a stick of incense. In that way, I "lock in" the intention and message from my daily glyph reading.

The Best Place for Your Anam Glyph Altar

There is no right or wrong place for an altar. There are only two rules for building an Anam Glyph altar:

1. Construct your altar in a space you resonate with, and that you designate as "sacred."

2. You must keep your altar clean and tidy, free from debris or clutter. Sometimes I fail at that, which is the reason I couldn't find the original eight Glyphs after the visit from my mother. Lesson learned. My altar is neat, tidy, and dust free now. No matter what else you do in your sacred practice, it's important when you construct an altar that you respect it. Cleanliness is a sign of respect.

There may be particular deities you wish to honor at your altar. Some may want to place on their altar an image of a particular Goddess, or one of an Earth deity.

Your altar may be large or small, and may be located indoors or out. Outside altars can be fashioned from earth, stones, or natural rock formations, and are often found in natural caves, or in hollows of trees and forks of branches. I know the Ant Tribe often use pink pebbles from the River Kwa as altars. And I'm familiar with a Tower of Giraffes who create their altars on the tops of Camel Thorn Trees, from which they hang offerings of tropical fruits fermented in orange blossom mead. Osiris, my old Jackalope friend, dug an altar right into his warren.

I have an altar in my abode especially built by a team of Saki monkeys from Bo Bo Construction Company. It's perhaps forty inches in diameter, and is covered in a green cloth that Lacy, an Orb Weaver spider, crafted from silk of her own abdomen.

How to Interpret the Anam Glyphs

When you choose a Glyph, relax and let your heart open to its gift. I undergo a grounding process before reading the Glyphs. After my morning bath in the River Kwa, I call on the house squirrels to bring my Glyphs to me and I stand still for a few minutes with all four feet flat on the ground. Peggy A., because she is Hu Man, holds her bag of glyphs to her heart. I cannot do that since Hippos lack opposable thumbs, of course, but I close my eyes, focus on my love for the Goddess, and ask that she guide me in selecting the right Glyphs for my highest purpose, or for the highest purpose of the person I'm reading for. You may use any grounding ritual, or prayer, that works for you to help you better connect with your Glyphs. Ask your deity, your heart, or your innate spiritual nature for guidance.

If at first the Glyph or its message does not seem to match

your thoughts, questions, or present circumstances, consider that you may need to look at something else in your life right now. There are no wrong Glyphs, and you have not chosen your Glyph by mistake. There are no reversals in these Glyphs, either, meaning there is no reverse or contrary significance if you pull an upside down Glyph or pull one sideways. When upside down or sideways, what the symbol says is, "There is more than one way to look at this."

As you study the Glyph's image, what does it say to you? What comes into your mind or heart? It could be that the symbol reminds you of something or someone in particular. If so, that is important. It could be you believe a literal translation of the symbol is significant — for example, no matter what the documented interpretation tells you, Waterfall to you may literally mean that you need to drink more water, swim for exercise, or vacation near a waterfall. Trust your inside wisdom, and go with your gut and your heart in interpreting and understanding the meaning of the Anam Glyphs. We cannot stress this enough: What is important is how these stones inspire you.

Ways to Use Your Anam Glyphs

There are several ways to use the Glyphs. For your convenience, we have provided a few suggestions, but you are free to use your creative mind in working with the Glyphs in any way that makes sense to you. Peggy A. has an Earth friend who uses them to energize specific flower essence remedies. Others may choose to use them as a talisman. Another way to use them is to locate one among the thirty-two you are particularly drawn to and claim it as your personal power symbol. You can carry your symbol with you, wear it as jewelry, keep it on your altar, or put its image on your business cards, or web page. I've a good friend, a rhinoceros, who asks her house chimp each morning to tie her personal glyph to her horn with a bright red ribbon. What a fashionable way to carry a stone or card!

When you choose your Glyphs, if you lack opposable thumbs, enlist the help of a troodon or gorilla to pull them blindly from a bag or bowl, or lay them all face down, mix them, and simply select each at random for you. If you are Hu Man, or a Rendazian with opposable thumbs, you can do that for yourself, of course. Another way to select a Glyph is to place them all right side up. Choose your stones or cards according to which of the Glyphs you are most drawn to.

Your Anam Glyphs have their own energy, and in their own way they are alive and aware. The Glyphs do not like to be near electronic devices, such as computers, television sets, electrical sockets, Crystal Interfaces, microwaves, or under harsh lights and fluorescents. They prefer to be kept in a quiet place. They perform best and are most happy when they live near plants and flowers, near candles and crystals, or things from the natural world such as rocks, seashells, and drift wood. Keep them in their own special bag, or box, something attractive and colorful, and preferably made of natural materials such as cotton, silk, or hemp. Alternately, store them in a lovely box or pretty bowl made of wood, glass or ceramic materials. They do not like metal much, but precious metals such as silver or copper are fine.

Once in a while, when the two moons, Lady Luz and Lady Beth are full, I spread my Anam Glyphs on a cloth under the moonlight to energize them. On Earth, of course, you've only one nameless moon, but it will do the trick. Use them outside now and again to allow them to soak up sunlight, and experience the wind, rain, or snow.

Talk to your Glyphs. Greet them in the morning. Say good night to them before you fall asleep. Thank them. The better care you take of your Anam Glyphs, the more blessings they bestow upon you in return. Use your Glyphs often. The more you use them, the happier they are, and the more valuable information you will receive from them

How to craft your own set of Glyphs

Creating your own set of Anam Glyphs makes the process a personal experience from selecting the medium, to inscribing the symbols, to using your own set of Glyphs for the first time.

There are no hard and fast rules, but here are a few guidelines that may be of help:

1. Select natural materials. If you choose bark or wood be sure to ask permission of the tree unless you are using a felled branch, or taking from a tree that has passed into the arms of the Goddess. Seeds, walnut husks, or glass make wonderful glyphs. Bone is okay, too, but please, harvest only bone from shed antlers, and such. You may also draw the images on cards. I crafted my set from smooth stones I found in the River Kwa where I bathe every day. We hippos have a profound connection to rivers, making my Glyph set especially meaningful.

2. When searching for materials look with your heart rather than your head. When seeking to create my Glyphs, I got down on all four knees at the river bank, and examined each stone until I found those that "spoke" to me. It took a long time, moons and moons, for me to locate the exact right thirty-two stones for my set.

3. The size of the Glyphs matter not, but you have to create something you can easily handle, so not too big or too small. For me, six-inch wide stones worn smooth by running water work best, but I had to create

smaller glyphs because my squirrels must be able to pull the stones for me, and their tiny paws cannot handle anything large. I found, with their assistance, stones in about one inch diameter, flat on one side, reddish in color to match the soil of the riverbanks, and that of the dirt found in the vegetable gardens and beneath the hazelnut bushes of the hippo compound. Most Hu Mans will create Glyphs the size of an Earth coin, perhaps that of an American quarter. Others prefer to inscribe the symbols on cards. I know large species, such as mastodons, orcas, and some dinosaurs who fashion their glyphs from boulders. You do want your Glyphs to be of consistent feel, size, and heft, though.

4. Once you've collected all thirty-two pieces, ask your deity or the Goddess to bless each before you draw, paint or scratch the symbol. The symbols are simple lines and circles, easy for anyone, Hu Man or not, to recreate them. A baby otter could manage it.

5. When you've created the symbols on all thirty-two glyphs, bathe them in a sacred stream or river to cleanse them of any residual toxic energy, or at the very least, soak them for at least fifteen Earth minutes in clean water sprinkled with a pinch or two of ocean salt. Make certain the water covers the stones. If you are using cards, consecrate them by bathing them in the light of a new moon.

How To Cast Your Glyphs

This section shares some ways to cast your Glyphs; however, you are not bound by the suggestions below. Feel free to invent your own way of throwing or casting your stones, or drawing your cards. Our imagination is a magnificent and powerful creative instrument. The Anam Glyphs encourage you to use yours!

Possible Spreads: Anam's Journey

This reading gives you a snapshot of how you are progressing during your life's journey, and gives you insight into the direction you are moving toward at this moment in time.

Choose three Glyphs, one at a time. Select them blindly and randomly. The first one you choose represents your "Current Evolution." It gives you clues about your soul's progression *to this point*, where you are *right now*, and how you have evolved up to *this exact moment*. Place it on your divining cloth or surface face up.

The second one you select is "Anam's Direction." It holds information as to the next steps in your evolvement, and may give you an idea of what actions you can take to assist your soul's growth providing you remain on your current path. Place it on the divining cloth to the right to the first one. No matter how unseemly, there is a relationship between the first two Glyphs. Seek and discover that relationship. Also, look to see which of the two is stronger for you, which resonates for you more deeply. That is a clue as to what you need to focus on.

The final Glyph is your "Destination" or "Destiny." It indicates where you are headed if you remain on your current path. Place the Destiny Glyph between the other two but slightly above them so that the three form a triangle. The reason for this is that your Glyphs are in some manner related, and putting them in a triangle rather than in a straight row gives you a better picture of how they are connected. A row has a beginning and an end; a triangle, like a circle, has no beginning and no ending.

Read the interpretation of the first stone starting to the left, then the second one to the right, and finally, the Destiny Glyph. Study the Glyphs you have pulled, and put together the elements of each, creating for yourself a unique picture of the direction you see yourself moving in.

You can embark on a Soul's Journey any time you want, and as often as you choose. However, if your *Anam's Journey* readings are too close together, you may receive conflicting information, which you might find confusing, or you may be overwhelmed with information. We recommend you allow some time to pass — ninety days or more, between *Anam's Journey* readings to allow yourself time to evolve, so that you develop a clearer and more complete picture of your soul's progression as it continually adjusts and changes direction. Meanwhile, pull a daily Glyph before embarking on *Anam's Journey* again.

Anam's Journey Spread: Destiny (or destination)

Current Evolution, Anam's Direction

Discovering Your Personal Symbol

This reading is a way to discover your Personal Symbol. Study the Glyphs' interpretations. One will stand out for you more than the others. Find the one that creates within you a sense of connection. That will be the Glyph that your soul resonates with at the highest vibration, and that becomes your personal symbol, your talisman.

An alternate way to seek your Personal Symbol is the *Radical Trust* method. Simply pull one glyph and be willing to accept with certainty that the meaning attached to the Glyph is yours.

Answering Questions and Providing Insights

With a question or issue clearly in mind, pull a Glyph. Read its entire meaning. Even though the answer may not be initially clear, or may not make complete sense, search for clues and patterns in either the symbol or the text accompanying the symbol, then you can combine those clues and follow the path they lead you toward in discovering your answer. You should not have to stretch too far to receive a response to your question. If it is very difficult to find a response that matches your question, leave it alone for a while. Go back to it in a day or two and try again.

If you are looking for a "yes" or "no" type of response, pull a Glyph and read its meaning, including the Exercise. The first time you perceive one of these words or phrases, the Glyphs have given you your answer:

- Yes,
- No,
- Perhaps,
- Maybe,
- Not necessarily,
- For certainty,
- Certainly,
- Surely,
- Indeed,
- Not now,
- Not yet,
- You have more work to do,
- Now is the time,

- Now is not the time,
- Move forward,
- Change direction,
- After a proper period of gestation,
- Patience,
- Definitely.

The only two invalid responses are "never" or "forever" because those two concepts are an illusion. These words do not even appear in the interpretations for any of the Anam Glyphs.

> *Special Note: What if you do not find an answer? Pull only one more Glyph, but this time, restate your issue or question. You may not have been clear in your initial request. The more specific and the more definite you are in your petition, the more easily you will find your answer. Do not continue to pull one Glyph after another to receive a specific answer in hopes for the response you want. If for any reason, you do not feel you have received a solid response to your question, let it go for now. The Goddess may not be ready to respond to you, or a decision on the other side may not have yet been made, or perhaps now is not the right time. With complete trust that all will work out fine, accept the answer the Glyphs give to you, and move on.*

The Anam Glyphs' Daily Gift

Consciously ask the Anam Glyphs to show you your purpose for the day, and to reveal what you most need to focus on during the twenty-four hours after your reading. Peggy A. chooses one Glyph and reads its meaning. Within the symbol she receives a message that guides her through her day. She carries the Glyph with her to remind her of what she is meant to focus on or do. As previously mentioned, I prefer to pull three. I read the messages, imprint them in my mind, and leave them on my altar to energize through the day.

Pulling a Glyph, or three, first thing every morning is a good daily practice because with consistent use, the Glyphs will help you to maintain your focus on love, service to others, kindness, your relationship to the Universe, your connection to nature, and your own divine qualities. The Anam Glyphs have great blessings to bestow upon you. Record how the circumstances of your life steadily improve as you connect with the Glyphs daily.

Try These Games for Fun

Throw an Anam Glyph party with one person designated as host. All you need to play this game is three or more people, a set of Anam Glyphs and their messages. If you can, host your Anam Glyph party outside in a lovely setting. If not, someone's abode is fine, too.

Game I: Collective Consciousness

1. To play the "Collective Consciousness" game, beginning with the host, each of the participants pulls one Glyph blindly and randomly from a bag or bowl, ensuring that no one else can see the symbol on the Glyph. The guests write down the name of the Glyph they pull, or recreate its image on a piece of paper, or drawn in soil, making sure no one else sees it. Then they put the Glyph back into the bag or bowl and pass it to the next person who does the same.

The reason the guests do not hold onto the actual Glyph is because it may be that two people will pull the same one, meaning that their life's purposes are closely aligned, or there is a message common to two or several people the Anam Glyphs want them to hear.

2. Once all guests have chosen their Glyphs, the host reads the messages for each person's Glyph out loud to everyone.

3. After each person receives their information from the Glyph, the host facilitates discussion about how the messages relate to one another, and how everyone's life's purpose is connected to the others'. How many of the participants pulled the same Glyph? If there are two or more who have pulled the same image, they may consider a partnership or alliance of some kind. They certainly do have things in common worth exploring. Discuss the ways the Anam Glyphs link all of you. If each participant is willing to share openly with the group, they can talk about the personal meaning of their Glyph. They might share with the group how the stone's message applies to their current life circumstances, or

what personal insights they receive from the symbol or its meaning. The clues are found in the symbols on the Glyphs themselves, or in their interpretations.

Played with in this way, the Anam Glyphs serve to bring groups of people together into a common purpose, and to strengthen bonds of friendship and kinship. This is also a fun game to play with family members! With this game, you gain valuable insights as to why you were born into a certain family, or why you may have attracted a particular group of friends.

Game II: Guess Your Best

Another fun party game: the party host or hostess gives each participant a few minutes to read the messages of each Glyph, and make an association between the Glyphs and the other participants. The idea is to guess each participant's Glyph. Record your guesses, but do not reveal them to anyone just yet. In making your guesses about someone, consider the person's personality, their talents, their current profession, their tastes, their likes and dislikes, their history, and their current skills. Each person pulls a Glyph, and then it's time for sharing!

With the group, compare what you have written down or guessed with what the Anam Glyphs say about each participant. Is there any relationship at all between what you wrote and the other persons' Anam Glyph's messages? This exercise can stimulate interesting conversation, and provides insights into how well you know your friends and family.

CONSULTING THE ANAM GLYPHS

Acknowledging and Using Your Power

The Anam Glyphs will serve you in many ways, but while working with them, remember always that you are in control of your own destiny. You are an awe-inspiring, remarkable, and astounding being. As such, you are your own prophet, your own Cybil, your own oracle. You have the ability to determine how to use your infinite wisdom in conjunction with the Glyphs to determine the right actions to take so that you may manifest your dreams and desires. In doing so, you have the incredible capability to help others realize their dreams and desires as well. You are more powerful and wise than you can imagine and the Universe is truly humbled by who you are.

My dear friend, and one of my spiritual counselors, Beard, is a banyan tree thousands of years old. He often says: "There is no magic more powerful than that of our own making." The Anam Glyphs are magic, in that they help us to know the unknowable. So, in using your Glyphs, you are indeed making your own strong magic.

And now you can begin interpreting The Anam Glyphs!

ALMA

NEW BEGINNINGS, BRIGHT PROMISE

Description
Alma looks like a sunrise over ocean waves or hills. The Glyph is represented by a half sun with rays reaching out into the sky.

Origin
Alma means "spirit" or "soul" in Spanish. The symbol of this Glyph represents a sunrise.

Interpretation
If you receive Alma, the dark night is falling behind you now, and a new day with all of its bright new promise is yours. This is the time for new beginnings, a fresh start. If you are considering a life change, entering into a new relationship, or are embarking on a new business or creative venture, receiving the soul-light of Alma puts you on notice that it is time for you to shift your dreams, ideas and plans into action. Go for it!

If you are experiencing emotional pain, sadness, despair, or any other darkness in your life, when Alma makes an appearance, rest assured that a new day is at last dawning with its healing light and warmth. You are entering a time of celebration and joy because your soul is now freely accepting the spirit-light of Alma here to assist you in defeating your darkness, your fears and lack of awareness. In partnership with the sun, light is now streaming into your spirit. Rejoice, but be aware that Alma is also a call to action. As you joyfully and gratefully accept new light in your life, you must also become as the spirit of the dawn, shining your own light into the Universe, sharing it with others. Imagine that your heart is the sun, and each time you encounter another person, consciously shine the rays of your heart-light outward to them. Notice how others respond to your warmth. Count how many people smile at you today.

And, never take Alma for granted. Every night when we retire to our beds, or our sleeping straw, we trust the suns will rise. But, seldom do we take the time to acknowledge the morning sun's life-giving warmth and light. If you accept the sunlight with a grateful heart, wonderful spiritual light and blessings (both tangible and intangible) will multiply for you with each day.

Sometimes a person comes into your life who represents Alma. My close friend, Lizzy, is that for me. She's always a bright spot in my life, and is forever upbeat and positive. Sometimes, when I pull Alma, I know it's time for me to take a walk to the Mastodon compound for a visit with Lizzy.

Exercise

Wake up one morning before dawn to actually experience the glory of a new day. Savor the pale light of the sun's rays spreading over the plains, the meadows, the mountains, the water, your home, the rooftops of your neighborhood, or skyline of your city, first a pale silvery blue, then pink, and finally, golden yellow. Little by little each day, sunlight makes its appearance in your life. Feel the new morning air, crisp and clean. Hear the birds as they awaken. As you witness the miracle of the sunrise, fill your heart with its light, its infinite spirit. As the new dawn emerges, open your heart to experience feelings of deep gratitude for the promise that each new day brings to you. Whether indoors, or outdoors, an important thing to do first thing when you awake each day is face the sun and count your many blessings out loud. As you consciously practice gratitude, and share your light with others, you will become infused with a new spiritual awakening and light-consciousness, and very soon you notice even more gifts coming into your life. Try this morning affirmation: "I am a Child of Light. Today I choose to live in the light and share my light with others."

ANGELWING

DIVINE PROTECTION, SAFETY

Description

Angelwing is represented by a single outstretched bird wing, or that of an angel.

Origin

This is the first of our Power Stones. Angels and helpful winged spirits exist in both the Earthian and Rendazian cultures, and have long been associated with protection. A magnificent winged being, so eclipsed by its own brilliant light I could not tell exactly what it might be, appeared to me in a vision. I dared not look upon it full on for I may have been struck blind. In my peripheral vision, I recognized its shape as a giant winged tabby cat, or an albino sasquatch, or an androgynous Hu Man over seven feet tall. I knew in my heart I had beheld a magical, divine spirit, an angel, that had appeared to let me know I my fears are unfounded. Angelwing would become one of the most powerful Anam Glyphs.

Interpretation

When you attract Angelwing, know you are under divine protection, and you truly have nothing to fear from life. Some events can create an illusion that we are unsafe, or may even trigger anxiety. There are also those among us plagued by fears we cannot explain, or which may seem illogical. Or, perhaps we have experienced situations when we were threatened or harmed, and now find it difficult to overcome our memory of fear associated with the incident.

When you see Angelwing, know that nothing can truly harm you, because no matter what happens to your physical self, your soul-self is always safe. You and your loved ones are divinely guided, and are protected by the loving wings of angels.

When you enter into an uncertain situation, or feel afraid, call on the protection of the angels or loved ones who have passed into the arms of the Goddess, and know they will appear at your side in an instant. You are protected, dear one, and the wings of powerful angels embrace you, and those you love always. When you need to know that angels are nearby, close your eyes and allow yourself to feel the soft, nearly imperceptible, brushing of a wing against your cheek.

Peggy A. says her mother, who long before passed into the arms of the Goddess, comes to her in her thoughts and dreams. She envisions her mother as Angelwing, and is much comforted by the presence of her mother's spirit. "When I pull Angelwing," She says, "I believe it's Mom's way to let me know she loves me and is watching over me."

Exercise

When you retire to your sleeping pillows for the evening, before you fall asleep, imagine the enormous white wings of a compassionate angel enfolding your home, and loved ones within a beautiful, protective embrace. Envision a big blue angel standing guard in your bedroom or at the door of your abode. When you travel, imagine a protective angel sitting with you in the passenger's seat or behind you, or even riding on the hood or roof of your AutoMobile machine or, of the wagon your camel pulls. When you travel by air or sea imagine an enormous pink angel with her arms wrapped around your ship or plane, guiding all to safety.

CÚPLA

RELATIONSHIPS, BUSINESS PARTNERSHIPS, ROMANTIC LOVE

Description

The symbol of Cúpla is represented by a horizontal "S" shape, with both ends terminating in simple opposing spirals, one spiraling in one direction, the other spiraling in the opposite direction.

Origin

Cúpla is the Irish Gaelic word for "twins." The name is closely related to the English word "Couple" and sounds a bit like "Cupid." This Glyph has within it elements of our inner male/female balance, known by the Taoist as Yin and Yang, the dual nature that resides within us all. Cúpla is symbolic of our relationship to ourselves, our relationship to the divine, and our romantic, business, and other personal relationships.

Interpretation

Call upon Cúpla when you wish to strengthen your relationship with all aspects of self. It is important to know that you cannot have a great relationship with anyone else until you first forge a great relationship with yourself.

Another aspect of Cúpla is the revitalization and ignition of romantic relationships. Perhaps you are in a relationship, or marriage, that is in need of a renaissance. Maybe you've been with the same partner for a long while and want to rekindle a little romance and fun. Perhaps you are in a friendship you would like to move to the next level. If so, invoke Cúpla.

Or, perhaps you are on your own and would like to enter into a romantic relationship. Much like Cupid, the cherubic angel of love, Cúpla serves as a mystical matchmaker whose purpose is to bring people together into romantic union. If you want to attract a loving mate, and enjoy a healthy, caring, relationship, Cúpla is here to serve you. Notice how the twin spirals are connected and mirror one another, yet still remain separate. Two people who join together in love, and pool their separate resources, their individual experiences and unique talents, create something together far more beautiful and greater than the sum of the relationship's parts. The healthiest and most loving relationships are those in which both parties support each other's dreams and aspirations, nurture one another's talents and gifts, and respect one another's individuality, all the while enjoying life together to the fullest. This is the kind of romantic relationship that Cúpla can help you to attract or create.

Yet another aspect of Cúpla is that of a professional union, a business partnership. If you are in a business relationship, it's time to take a step back and evaluate the association. Is the business union balanced and fair? Are all parties being served by the relationship? Or, do you need to attract a new partner into a business venture? Cúpla helps to strengthen or clarify existing business relationships, and will help you to attract the right partners.

If you are in a relationship or partnership that is hurting you, or is crushing your spirit, or is in any way abusive rather than nurturing, Cúpla implores you to reexamine your need to be in the relationship. When we are in hurtful relationships, whether they be personal or business in nature, they drain our energy and distract us from being able to fulfill our life's purpose, our destiny, our higher mission. In these cases, rely on this Glyph for inner guidance and assistance. Cúpla stands ready to give you the strength to help you change, or terminate a relationship that hurts you, or no longer serves your highest good.

Exercise

Purchase three new candles. In this instance, the candles and colors we use are based on Feng Shui principles. Purchase a pink candle for love or kinship, a black candle for Yin energy, the female aspect of self, and a red candle for Yang energy, the male aspect of self. On a piece of paper, write your relationship request. For example, you might write this: "I wish to build a stronger union between myself and the Universe," or, "I wish to attract a loving partner who is intelligent, wise, kind and who is financially independent." Or "I wish for renewed joy, intimacy and affection, and more harmony in my current relationship." Or, "I ask the way to help create change in my current relationship to transform it into a loving union, or be given the courage to walk away." Another request may be "I wish to attract a business partner who will be instrumental in the success of my current venture."

Be specific, using names when you can. If your partner's name is Sally, actually write her name. The more specific your details, and the stronger your intention for creating a fulfilling relationship, the more powerful your request.

To the left, place the black candle. To the right, place the red. In the middle, but in *front* of the other two, place the pink candle on top of the paper on which you have scribed your wishes for improving or attracting a relationship. In front of the pink candle, place Cúpla. You may also add to the arrangement a crystal, a photograph, or anything that has meaning to you. Light the candles. Seal an image of Cúpla within your mind. Then allow yourself to fully experience all those feelings you would have if your wishes as you have written them had already materialized. Allow the fire to burn the three candles completely down. Over the next ninety days, notice what manifests for you within the sphere of your relationships.

CYNN

FAMILY, COMMUNITY RELATIONSHIPS

Description

The symbol for Cynn is a straight line, overlaid by two lines like a sideways "V" mid-way that form a point like an arrow, overlaid again by a curved line that resembles a pregnant belly. Getting this drawing exactly right is unimportant. What is important is that the three lines, curved, straight, and those at angles, touch one another as in a family unit.

Origin

Cynn is the Anglo-Saxon word for "family." This Glyph signifies the bonds shared by family, both biological and chosen, and community.

On Rendaz, our planetary symbol for a traditional hetero "family" is a straight horizontal line (male), overlaid by the symbol of a pregnant belly (female). In The Anam Glyphs, we've taken this symbol one further step and have included the connecting lines shaped in a sideways "V" to symbolically codify the Yin and Yang elements.

Interpretation

When you receive Cynn, you may simply need to pay closer attention to your family and community relationships. There is abiding joy in the unity and love that a family shares. If you are part of a loving, close biological family, than you are truly blessed. However, Cynn also reminds us that family is not necessarily about biology. We can choose our family. Throughout our time on this planet, people enter and leave our lives with whom we form tight kinships. Familial love and powerful bonds can be forged between people who are not related to one another in any way by blood ties, or who may not even always be with us throughout our entire current lifetime. It is not uncommon for any of us to have many brothers and sisters who are not related to us by the occasion of birth. It is not uncommon for a child to have many mothers besides her birth mother. Cynn says those dearest to us may not share a common bloodline with us, but they share a common heart line with us. All it takes to be a family are two or more people who contribute to a common love and a feeling of kinship for one another.

Cynn says it's particularly important for us to recognize that we are all part of a Hu Man or Rendazian family just as we are all connected to every living being throughout the Universe. Who do you count among your family members? Right now is the time for you to recognize your place in your family, to feel your family's loving arms around you, and to be grateful for those in your life who love you, no matter who they may be, and no matter who you are. Cynn says you are never alone.

When you receive Cynn, it could also be the time for you to reconnect with a family member or friend who you have been estranged from, or are currently angry with. Cynn has great power to help mend broken relationships. Is there someone close to you who you have not spoken to in a long while or who you may have lost contact with? Cynn has made an appearance in your life to help you to reconnect with them.

Whenever you are feeling lonely, have lost contact with someone who is dear to you, are struggling with a broken familial relationship, or are in need of community, call on Cynn and you will receive warm and nurturing support.

Special Note from Peggy A. Wheeler

Cynn is a precious Glyph to me because my own biological family is scattered. I've very little family with whom I share a bond, and must find my family among my friends. Cynn reminds me that perhaps I'm not quite as alone as I imagine myself to be. I carry an image of Cynn with me wherever I go.

Exercise

Draw a picture of your family as you might have when you were a bubbit. Who is in the picture? Are the figures related to you by birth? Are they Hu Man, Rendazian, or spirit? What are their names? Make sure one of the family members in the picture is you. Or, create a collage from photos and impressions of your family members. Again, make sure you are represented in the collage, too. Where is everyone in relationship to everyone else in the picture? Where is everyone standing or sitting? Put your family picture or collage somewhere where people usually put their family photos. Look at it often to remind yourself that you *are* part of a family.

DJINN

CROSSROADS, DIRECTION, NEW PATHWAYS

Description

To create the Djinn symbol draw an X terminated in arrows at each point outward so that there are four arrows. Between each of the intersections of the X, put a small circle or dot so that you've four dots total.

Origin

This Glyph is named for the Wiccan Elemental King of Fire. Djinn are also fire elementals in Islamic myths, and in some cultures, they are also known as Genies. The Glyph itself is an ancient one found in many cultures, particularly in American Native pictographs. In this context, Djinn's meaning is primarily a symbol of a transformational crossroad, and/or a need for guidance from your own personal "genie."

Interpretation

When you receive Djinn, you are faced with the possibility you have outgrown the life you are now living, and it may be the time for you to change direction. The good news is that Djinn, serving as your personal Genie guide, tells you that there are no wrong decisions, no mistakes, and all possibilities are good ones.

The arrows on the four points serve as clear indications that whatever path you choose, it will take you directly where you want to be or need to go. The "focal points" between each arrow keep you focused on your purpose. The message of Djinn is you are capable of making the right decision or discovering the perfect resolution to any problem you are currently experiencing. Have faith that the right decisions, followed by the exact right action for you will come to you effortlessly, and everything will work out just fine for you and everyone else involved.

If you are having trouble making a decision, or feel "stuck" in your life, rub an imaginary magic lamp and summon the firepower of Djinn to help you. Once you've made a decision, go for it with gusto and passion, and trust in the outcome.

Exercise

Sit in a quiet place with a pad and pencil nearby. Focus on an actual image of the Djinn Glyph, or hold an image of Djinn in your mind. Direct your full attention to your heart-center, inhaling and exhaling from your heart until you feel that your heart is breathing instead of your lungs.

Ask yourself what you are confused about, what decisions you are struggling with, what problems in your life are you having difficulty resolving, what life change do you need to make in order to support new growth, which path do you need to follow? When you ask these questions, if you sense a tightening or pressure, or any uneasiness or even a slight shift in your gut, solar plexus, or in your chest, know that you have reached an important crossroad in your life. Keep your attention on your heart, and your focus on Djinn. Ask the Glyph what the right action is for you. Djinn will answer you. Immediately, no matter what comes to you, write down the answer. Know with surety that this is the correct answer because you have connected with your most powerful innate wisdom. It is from that wise place that all right answers reside. With Djinn's assistance, all decisions you make, actions you take, and paths you choose, will yield the outcome best for your good.

DREAM LIZARD

THE IMPORTANCE OF DREAMS

Description

The symbol for Dream Lizard is a simple line drawing of a common lizard.

Origin

In many Earthian and Rendazian cultures, lizards are long associated with the dream world, and with mutability. Lizards are particularly revered in Australian aboriginal culture. On Rendaz, we often pay our lizards an abundance of glowseeds to professionally interpret our dreams, and the lizards are seldom wrong.

While walking near a stream with some good friends, we stopped to rest and the lizards came out, many of them, a lime skink juvenile gave me the inspiration for including Dream Lizard in the Glyphs.

Interpretation

It is through our dreams that our subconscious communicates with us. Dreams are also the way that those in the "other worlds" relay important messages to us. When Lizard makes an appearance, it means you must pay close attention to your dreams, especially those that speak of change, adaptability, mutability and transformation. Your dreams are talking to you, and they are powerful.

Lizards also represent transformative change. There are even lizards, such as the chameleon, that change color depending on where they are so as to become nearly invisible. These reptiles quickly sense and adapt to their surroundings better ensuring their survival. Like the butterfly, snake, frog and dragonfly, lizards symbolize powers of renewal. Some lizards, much like snakes, climb out of their old skin leaving it behind in one piece, growing stronger, quicker, and more beautiful with each shedding and subsequent renewal.

Through recalling your dreams and paying attention to their messages, you receive insights to support your evolution, and help you to hone your intuitive power and gain spiritual strength. Pay attention to your dreams, and you can become like the Dream Lizard, more intuitive, flexible, mutable, adaptable, spiritually stronger, and more inwardly beautiful.

Exercise

Keep the Dream Lizard Glyph beside your bed. Before you fall asleep at night, affirm that you will remember your dreams. Call on Dream Lizard for his help. As you retire for the evening, a meditation or an affirmation to ask that you recall your dreams is good practice. Try this: "Tonight, I will sleep deeply and restfully. Tomorrow I will awake clear-headed and refreshed. I will recall all of my dreams in complete and vivid detail." Keep a pad and pen by your bed, and before you rise in the morning, spend a moment to remember your dreams. Write them down immediately. Throughout the day think about them; be aware of their messages. Thank Dream Lizard for his assistance.

FEOH CUP

IMPROVING FINANCIAL MATTERS, MONEY

Description

The symbol of this Glyph is a short, footed goblet with three lines "pouring" into it from the top, right side. The lines represent a flow of money.

Origin

Feoh means currency in the Anglo-Saxon language. When I imagine money, instead of piles of Rendazian Glowseeds, stacks of paper currency, or gold bars, a magic chalice comes to mind. The goblet is continually filled with prosperity, and the holder can take from it whenever they desire, as often as they desire, yet the cup is never empty.

Interpretation

When you receive Feoh Cup, financial issues are at hand. Perhaps you feel a sense of lack, or are stressed financially, or you have been worried because it seems there is not enough money. Feoh Cup is a sign of plenty. Notice how the cup fills with a constant flow of prosperity. Receiving this glyph is a message for you to cease your worrying and fear over money. Feoh Cup is your assurance that you will work out your financial issues, and there will be *enough* money.

Be open to the opportunities that come your way to earn income. As long as you are grateful and remain focused on abundance supported by action, the way will come to you to earn or attract the money you desire. No matter what your current circumstance, it's important for you to believe that you truly live in a prosperous universe, and there is enough for everyone.

If you want to generate more money in your life, practice gratitude for what you already have. Count your blessings daily. Visualize receiving money, a check for a large sum of money, or cash, or landing a great job that pays more than you've ever earned. How does it feel to have all you need or want? Hold an image of the Feoh Cup in your mind, and ask for opportunities to earn money. Then be vigilant for the opportunities that life blesses you with.

Another important gift Feoh Cup gives is to remind artists that they, too, deserve an abundance of money. If you are an artist, and you struggle with financial issues, this is the time to completely release and reject the erroneous notion that you cannot ask for payment in exchange for the talents and the gifts you share with the world. If you are uncomfortable in asking for or receiving pay for your work, you create an imbalance, and in doing so you block your own abundance. Universal law states we must be in satisfactory exchange to keep the flow in circulation.

There is no nobility in being in poverty or suffering from lack. There is no romance in playing the role of the "struggling artist," or the long-suffering martyr. In fact, when you play these roles, rather than being perceived as generous and loving, the lack of worth you assign to your work and talents serves only to dilute the value of your gifts. When you are out of energetic exchange for your work, you risk losing your self-respect, as well as the respect of others, because you do not place a high value on what you offer. Furthermore, no one else can value or respect your talents if you do not value them yourself. As a result, when someone accepts your gifts without reciprocation, they do not benefit nearly as powerfully as they do when they pay in kind for your services or your art. Know that your gifts to the world are priceless, and it is your responsibility to generate and maintain energetic exchange. Know too, that the more prosperous you are, and the more you give to yourself, the more art you can create, the more good works you can do, and the more you can give to others. Artists, keep an image of Feoh Cup with you always to remind you to hold your talents in high regard, and to value your own worth.

"I like Feoh Cup the most," Peggy A. says.

"Why is that? Is it because you like money so much?"

"It's because I like wine so much, and this chalice reminds me of the one I drink my Pinot Noir from."

"Hahaha. Personally, I prefer a nice pail of sparkling honeysuckle mead, something I can really stick my muzzle into. But, I suppose a chalice of Hu Man wine is not too bad. Of course, in your case, as much wine as you drink one chalice won't do it anyway. You might as well drink it from a pail."

One, I suppose, can choose to fill Feoh Cup with wine, or money, or whatever they so desire!

Hint: If matters of abundance are at issue, or feelings of lack are present, also look to Waterfall for guidance.

Exercise

Try this affirmation: Five times a day or more and every time you begin to feel a sense of lack, proclaim aloud: "I have all that I need, and more, because I deserve to be prosperous. I accept and enjoy the many blessings I have right now, and I am grateful for the many blessings that the Universe continually provides to me. I attract prosperity continually, and gladly share what I have with others. The Universe is bountiful and generous. Many opportunities reveal themselves to me for earning and attracting money."

GREENLEAF

THE HEALER AND THE AFFLICTED, HEALING AND REGENERATION

Description

Greenleaf is symbolized by a line drawing of a leaf with prominent veins. Any photo or drawing of a green leaf from a deciduous tree will do nicely.

Origin

Look closely at any leaf from a deciduous tree and notice how its fine veins form intricate, delicate patterns. Although leaves from the same tree can appear very similar, there are no two leaves exactly alike. Peggy A. and I chose the leaf to be part of the Anam Glyphs because green leaves speak to us of spring, new growth, vibrant health, the unique beauty within each individual, and of cycles in nature.

Interpretation

The body, like the tree, is meant to renew itself, and with each cycle of its own nature, the body sheds its old cells and grows new, fresh, cells so that every seven or so years, our body re-grows itself. If you've been ill, Greenleaf is the bringer of health.

Each body cell, like a leaf to a tree, plays an important role in the health of the individual. As even the loss of one leaf makes a difference in the health of a tree, the loss of cells makes a difference in the health of the individual. If a tree loses too many of its green leaves prematurely, it will die. A person's body will die if it loses too many of its cells prematurely. The good news, renewal happens. When Greenleaf appears in your life, healing via regeneration is afoot, whether it be physical spiritual, or emotional.

Greenleaf tells you that to heal yourself; it's time to renew or make a fresh start in some way. Perhaps you need to let go of something that has limited your potential or your true nature. Perhaps the winter of depression, or the numbing coldness of despair has closed in around you, and you require the warmth of spring to lift your spirits and heal your heart.

If you feel as though your life has no purpose, or if you see yourself as ordinary and less than the beautiful and special wise being you are, call upon Greenleaf. Your outlook, your health, and your mood will begin to improve. If you are receptive, you will discover all you require to understand the seasons of your life, and cycle of rebirth into health, can be found in the simple Greenleaf — the promise of Spring, the warmth of Summer, the beauty of Autumn, the healing nature of the world. Greenleaf serves as a symbol of your own unique magnificence, your wholeness, and a reminder of the importance of your existence.

Greenleaf offers an important healing message. All that any Hu Man or Rendazian needs to heal the body is available to us in our Earthian and Rendazian plant life. Greenleaf says, "Look to the plants, to their roots, leaves, stems, and flowers, for healing yourself and others." Take advantage of modern medicine, but as much as possible, use natural means for healing yourself. Your body will be grateful to you for it. If you've suffered from illness and physical pain, Greenleaf is the Glyph you most need.

Exercise

When you are feeling sick or tired, in need of healing, go out among the leaves and study them. Gather leaves from many trees and put them in a bowl or plate in a special place of your home, or on your altar. If the season is not right for gathering leaves, or you live in a climate where there are few or no green leaves, buy a leafy green plant and keep it in a special place. Make a habit of acknowledging the leaves of the plant every day with gratitude for the health-giving gifts and life's lessons Greenleaf teaches you.

HEARTHAND

HELPFUL PEOPLE, SUPPORT FROM FRIENDS AND ALLIES

Description

The symbol of Hearthand is a line drawing of an upraised open Hu Man hand with a heart in the palm.

Origin

In Rendazian society, the image of a single upraised paw, wing, or hand on someone's abode symbolizes a place where a traveler, a child, or lost being can expect help, shelter, and a meal. On Earth, the heart represents love and caring. What would be more fitting than to use a hand with a heart as a symbol of helping and caring?

Interpretation

When this Glyph shows itself to you, it is to remind you that helpful people surround you, and support you. Hearthand says friends, partners, and allies, visible and invisible act on your behalf and are interested in your highest good. They sustain you.

Hearthand says you do have friends, some you may not be aware of, and even more may appear in your life in the near future. You are put on notice that you will attract to you exactly the right people to help you to achieve your goals, and to help fulfill your life's purpose. You may meet someone casually who will connect you with a heart-centered person whose purpose it is to serve as an ally, muse, or catalyst for you. Whether you are conscious of them or not, you may know someone already who serves you in the role, perhaps a business acquaintance, a mentor, a teacher, a friend or a neighbor who is your ally, or will act as such when you need them, or who will introduce you to someone who will turn out to be very helpful to you in some unexpected way. And, you may have very specific loving unseen beings around you who will direct you to the people you need.

My hearthands are my friends, Samuel S. Goodwings, Lizzy, Calypso, Agnes, Applecheeks, and my spiritual mentors and teachers, Beard, and Lady Rhianna. To a different degree, my one and only Hu Man friend helper, Peggy A. Wheeler, is a hearthand. Who are yours?

Pay particularly close attention to the people around you now, and notice any new acquaintances entering your life over the next few months. Be vigilant of synchronicities, any amazing or unlikely "coincidence" that occurs within the sphere of your personal relationships, people who know one another from a different time or place, who share a common name or background, or have characteristics in kind with your biological family or ancestors. These are the people who have entered your life with their heart in their hand and have appeared in your life to help you in an obvious way, or in a subtle way you may not immediately notice. Be aware of any visitations in your dreams from those who have passed. They come to you in your visions and dreams to help you. You are surrounded by helpful people and entities who love you and care about you.

My mother, Sangrina, may her soul rest in the palm of The Goddess, often appears to me in my visions, and sometimes, my dreams. She guides me from the other side, and encourages me when I'm feeling low or worthless.

Exercise

Make a list of all the people you know in your life who have supported you or helped you in some way. Whether they are alive, or have crossed over, are currently in your life or have long moved on, express gratitude to each. If you are moved to do so, write each a letter or message, or call them, just to say "thank you for being there for me." If those who you wish to show gratitude to are no longer in your life, your "thank you" notes can be written, and placed on your altar to honor them, or put them in a fireproof container and burn them as an offering. The more gratitude you express and feel toward those who help you now, or who have helped you in the past, the more "Hearthands" you attract into your life.

MAAHE

THE TEACHER AND THE STUDENT, INTELLECT, KNOWLEDGE, EDUCATION

Description

The symbol of Maahe is a single line, with another single line at an angle so that the two lines appear as an arrow, only not touching.

Origin

Maahe means "Arrow" in the Cheyenne language. The shape of this Glyph represents a stylized arrowhead. To the indigenous people of North America, the arrow has symbolism relating to survival, and the point could easily represent a sharp mind, a fast thinker, or a pointed intellect. An arrow can also symbolically "point the way" for someone uncertain of their path.

Interpretation

When you receive Maahe, you most likely have a quick mind, but you may not be using all of your knowledge or your intelligence in the best way. Maahe says education, knowledge, and intellect play an important role in your life. It is possible you are currently a student, or it may be that you are being guided to seek additional education. You could also be a teacher or instructor in some discipline, or you are meant to teach.

Have you been thinking about going back to school to finish a degree? Have you been talking about learning a foreign language? Do you wish you could play the piano? Have you been thinking about taking a home study course in herbal studies? Or, perhaps, you are striving to learn more about your own nature, your spirituality. If so, Maahe says now is your time to study and learn. You would be well served to pursue additional education, and you are able to grasp complicated concepts. But, you need to remain focused. Maahe is a powerful medicine for students because it keeps the student "on target" with their studies, and helps students focus on their goals.

You may already be a teacher, or Maahe may be pointing you in the direction of being an educator or teacher because the other message this Glyph shares with you is this: once you have acquired knowledge, whether it be of an academic/mental nature, or artistic nature, you have a responsibility to use that knowledge in a way that serves others. In other words, Maahe says part of your gift to humanity is your fine mind, but you must share your knowledge, your intellectual and spiritual understanding with the world. You must develop your innate ability to teach and to educate. Seek the way to share your knowledge with others. Allow Maahe's arrow to point the way for you.

Exercise

If you are a teacher, a student, or are considering further education, carry the Maahe Glyph with you and touch it often. Put this Glyph on your desk where you study and read, or near your computer or Crystal Interface. Ask Maahe to give you focus and to help you stay on target.

If you are a teacher, carry the Glyph with you and call upon its energy to point the way for you to best share your knowledge and use your knowledge for the good of others. If you are a student or a teacher, you will benefit by putting an image of Maahe in the northeast corner of your home in your study or office, anywhere where you attend to the business of learning or teaching. Near the Glyph, burn a yellow candle, the color of intellect and clarity, and a white candle, the Feng Shui color of the northwest. In the same corner as Maahe and the candles, place a small white bowl of sea salt to keep your energy, your chi, calm, clear and centered. The Northeast is the Feng Shui area for "motivation." Keeping this Glyph here will help you maintain focus and to increase energy.

Put a second image of Maahe on the northeast corner of your desk where you study or prepare for teaching. When you are working and your mind begins to wander, look at Maahe as a reminder that your work is important and you must stay on target.

MOONMAJICK

WISHES MANIFESTED THROUGH GODDESS ENERGY

Description

This Glyph is represented by a quarter moon, waxing, with three dots representing three stars between the points of the moon. If the moon were full, you would not see the stars.

Origin

Moonmajick is about fulfillment of wishes, feminine beauty and power, and is a symbol of the Great Goddess. The Moon Goddess appears under all of her names on nearly every continent in of Earth, and every Rendazian district. You will find her in Aztec, Polynesian, Mayan, Greek, Chinese, Egyptian, African, and Celtic mythology.

Interpretation

Moonmajick is here to help you to honor the feminine divine. In her different stages, the moon represents the triple goddess—the Maiden, The Mother, The Crone, comprising the feminine Holy Trinity. The Moonmajick Glyph depicts the waxing moon, the Maiden, the beautiful, strong, young girl-goddess who wants to share her gifts with you. She asks you to tell her what you want. She asks you to make a wish because your wishes can indeed come true. When Moonmajick comes into your life, she requires you to believe you deserve her blessings.

If you receive Moonmajick in a reading, or at any time you see an image of the waxing moon, she asks you to develop a closer relationship with the feminine aspect of the gods. It's time for you to introduce yourself to the Goddess, if you have already made her acquaintance, it's time to develop a more intimate relationship with her. Connect with the Goddess energy within you (and, yes, males have goddess energy within them, too), and be receptive to her blessings.

Every woman is a Goddess in her own right, by the way. If you are a woman, perhaps you simply need to become more aware of the divinity within yourself. If you are not a woman, you may need to honor the Goddess in the women in your life through acknowledging the blessings they bestow upon you. The more you seek the favor of the Goddess, the more she nurtures you and gifts you with her silvery light in return. "The Goddess is alive!" Moonmajick says, "Honor her and love her, and your wishes just might come true!"

Exercise

During the waxing phase of the moon, write a wish on a piece of paper. Place it under a crystal or white rock, and leave it outside where the moon(s) will shine on it for a full cycle. Face the moon(s) and thank her for her beauty, and for the blessings that she shares with us all. Ask her to grant your wish. For thirty days, write down the gifts and blessings that come into your life each day. Your wish could very well come true by then. If it doesn't, there will surely be many blessings that come into your life when you acknowledge the moon's beauty with a heart full of gratitude. The more you thank the energy of the moon and recognize her beauty, the more she gives back to you.

On Rendaz, we've several spiritual festival, over which my friend, the High Priestess, Rhianna, presides. Of all the festivals, the Luna Festival to honor our two moons, Lady Luz and Lady Beth, is my absolute favorite. It is then when I feel most aligned with Moonmajick. I ask my house squirrels to put the Glyph in my satchel to carry with me through the day of the festival as a way to honor the moons.

MOTHERBELLY

MOTHER ENERGY, GESTATION, BIRTH, MOTHERLY BLESSINGS

Description

The symbol of Motherbelly is a large "C," representing a full, pregnant belly.

Origin

Mother Belly is a Power Stone, and its full shape suggests that of impending birth and fecundity. In all cultures, particularly the Goddess culture on Rendaz, the full female belly filled with life is more sacred than an ancient tree or a High Priestess.

The pregnant abdomen represents new growth, birth and rebirth, maternal love and nurturing, and is symbolic of the roundness of our planets.

Interpretation

When you receive this Glyph, you are in tune with the Great Mother, She Who Brings Forth Life. Receiving Mother Belly means that after a proper period of gestation, nine months for Hu Mans, your plans, dreams, desires and ideas can at last be brought to life.

This is a time of joyful waiting for new growth and birth. However, the Mother Belly asks for your patience. Even though the Mother Belly is full and ready to bring forth life, she is not ready to give birth quite yet. All things that live must undergo a time of gestation before birth. If they emerge too soon, they will not survive outside of the womb, the chrysalis, or egg. Therefore, you are cautioned not to rush to "make things happen" before their time. When you receive Motherbelly, know it is proper to nestle into the great mother's womb and await your birth. It is time for introspection, peace, nurturing, and "mothering" of the self, as well as a critical time for the gestation of your ideas, dreams and desires. But, also know that while you are patiently waiting, the Great Mother is nourishing you, too, and you are greatly loved.

Since this symbol is one of motherhood, you might also explore its literal meaning. This may be the time to reach out to your own mother and to reconnect with her on an emotional or spiritual level. Even if your mother has passed over, this is a good time to summon her into your thoughts and feelings. If your mother and you—or your child and you—lack emotional intimacy, or if there is hurt between you, this is the time to forgive and to heal your critical mother-child relationships. If you do not know your mother well, this is the time to know her.

"...your mother's identity is key to your own identity... Failure to know your mother that is your position and its attendant traditions, history and place in the scheme of things, is failure to remember your significance, your reality, your right, your relationship to earth and society. It is the same as being lost—isolated, abandoned, self-estranged, and alienated from your own life."

— Paula Gunn Allen

Or, perhaps you are thinking of starting your own family. If so, Motherbelly is a sign that this could be the right time. No matter what, literally or figuratively, Motherbelly is an indication that something good will be born into your life.

Exercise

Thank your mothers. Sit quietly. Bring an image of your mother(s) into your mind. Your mother may be your birth mother, adoptive mother, stepmother, mother-in-law, aunt, older sister, or any older woman who has nurtured and helped to raise you who you think of as "Mother." You may have more than one woman in your life that you feel is your mother. Bring all of your mothers to your mind and ask them to stand in front of you.

Then bring an image of your planet to your mind. If she were Hu Man, or Rendazian, what would she look like? What color is her hair, her hide, her fur, her eyes? How old is she? Our planets are also our mothers. Take a moment to express to all of your mothers how grateful you are to them are for giving you life, and/or for helping you to grow, and for nourishing and sustaining you. Thank them for the many blessings, and lessons, and nurturing they have given to you. Embrace each one in turn and say to each, "Thank you for being my mother. I love you."

This is also a good time to actually call or write to your mothers to say, "Thank you for being my mother. I love you." Focus on your image of Mother Planet. While feeling love and gratitude for her, in a place that you feel is special, plant a small tree or a green bush, or cast wildflower seeds to thank her. If it is the wrong time of the year for planting, find a stone or small tree branch, and write on it "Thank you for being my mother. I love you," and place it on the ground somewhere special as your way to honor, and show love and gratitude to your mother planet.

OPENEYE

THE SEER, INNER VISION, SEEING TRUTH, PSYCHIC ABILITY

Description

The symbol for Openeye is a line drawing of an open eye without lashes or brows.

Origin

The meaning and origin of the Openeye Glyph is multifaceted. It represents the "third eye," which blesses us with great inner seeing, psychic power, and mystical wisdom. The eye is often thought to be the window of the soul, and represents our ability to see others and ourselves in a new light.

In Turkey, a blue glass eye is hung in people's homes and in their cars, or carriages, to ward off danger and evil. Openeye gives us the power to pierce the layers of fog and misconception that cloud our vision so we are finally able to see the truth of things.

Interpretation

When this Glyph appears, you are reminded that oftentimes "there is more than meets the eye" to any situation. Openeye's greatest gift to us is that it provides us with true insight, meaning the ability to see within.

When you pull this Glyph, it is a sure bet there is something you need to look at that you are currently not seeing. You are being prompted to nourish and use your psychic ability to see. Call upon the energy of Openeye if you desire the power to view anything with sharper clarity and a deeper understanding, and if you wish to cultivate your psychic "seeing." Those who focus on Openeye, and carry it with them, eventually develop a keen ability to see things that most others do not.

Exercise

Try to see something in your everyday world you have never noticed before. Look at your partner, friend, lover, spouse, work colleague. What color are their eyes? What have you never really looked at or noticed before about them? Look in your home, garden, neighborhood, town or city. What do you see today that you've never noticed or seen before? Take time to *see* the world. What new knowledge and wisdom do you gain from what you see? Pay attention. Before retiring for the evening, sit quietly for a few minutes and record everything you saw today that you'd never noticed before, and anything you might have learned from what you observed.

When you are relaxed, it is time to focus on your third eye—the space on your forehead between your eyes. Mentally or physically, tap that spot three times, and imagine that after the third tap your third eye opens wide and sees things within you and outside of you that you've never seen before. What does your third eye behold? Ask that your third eye magically allow you to see the truth of things. Once an image, an insight, or a vision comes to you, don't hesitate—immediately record what your third eye sees. You may be astonished at how clearly things come into focus for you.

PELÉ FIRE

PASSION, FIRE ENERGY, CHARGED EMOTION

Description

A triangle representing a volcano with fire spewing from the top is the symbol of Pele Fire.

Origin

Pelé Fire is named after the Earth Hawaiian Volcano Goddess, Pelé. She is expressive, powerful, and passionate. She destroys and she builds. The Pelé Fire Glyph is of an erupting volcano, and appears to those with passion, inspiration, and creative fire. When this Glyph appears in a layout, we are in the presence of abundant and powerful heart energy.

Interpretation

When Pelé Fire comes to you it can mean one of two things, either your passion drives you to excess, or you are in need of more passion in your life and your work. In balance, people with Pelé Fire energy are gregarious, energetic, outgoing people. Fun at parties, they are the "class clowns" as youngsters, who as adults become our great orators, comedians, our most passionate leaders and teachers.

You will find Pelé Fire people among the ecological warriors in Greenpeace and other activist groups on Earth. They are the heroes who risk their lives in service to our planets. They are also our world's optimists. They generally choose to see the bright side of life, and all the possibilities that life holds for them.

An erupting volcano has tremendous destructive power. People with an unbalanced overabundance of Pelé Fire are generally temperamental. They are said to have "fiery" or "explosive" personalities. The least little thing can set them off and they fly into a rage. Excess fire energy can trigger manic episodes, excessive jealousy, or even sometimes violent behavior. If too much Pelé Fire is centered in the first chakra, a person could be driven by their sexual urges, and may be promiscuous, or prone to engage in spontaneous, and even dangerous sexual activity.

Those with too much Pelé Fire can be overly passionate about their work to the point of obsession. They are also out of balance with their passion as it relates to their ideals and beliefs to the point of being overzealous because they feel obligated to impose their beliefs on everyone else. They are the ones who start wars and engage in war like behaviors. They are also among those people whose energy is so aggressive, or so "loud" and scattered, that you find it difficult to be around them for long periods of time. Children and adults on Earth and Rendaz with ADD or ADHD are often plagued by an overabundance of liver heat. When you receive this Glyph, you are being asked to look at those in your life you know (or have known) with an overabundance of Pelé Fire. What affect have these people had on your life? And, can you think of times when you have had to cope with an overabundance of Pelé Fire within yourself?

Without heart-centered passion life is dull and cerebral. A person with depleted Pelé Fire can lack energy or passion for anything. They have a very low sexual drive. They are often listless and depressed. People lacking Pelé Fire are not motivated to do much of anything. These are the people who constantly tell you that their lives or their work is "boring," and they do not care too much about themselves or others. Very often, they have a sour continence. People see them as "grumpy" or "dull" or both. They are humankind's complainers in life because these people view the world through a dim filter, and, therefore, have difficulty seeing the bright side of anything. People cannot be simultaneously passionately joyful, and miserably depressed. Given the choice, people lacking Pelé Fire tend to feel most comfortable being sad, down, and miserable, or they get "stuck" in that sad energy and have great difficulty escaping it. Is your energy sometimes low? If so, call upon Pelé Fire. She will spark things up quite a bit!

Invoke this Glyph when you need more passion in your life, or your work, or when you are feeling low emotionally and energetically. If you need more passion in your relationship, or desire to heat up your sexual energy, call on Pelé Fire. And, if you find that you have difficulty controlling your temper, or are very "excitable," impatient, and you feel your fire is out of control, ask her to use her feminine energy to help balance your passion.

Exercise

If your passion and energy are low, wear red and orange. Burn red, orange and bright yellow candles daily. Eat fiery foods such as chili, spicy Indian food, or Thai curry. Paint a wall or an entire room in your house in red or orange or gold. Listen to upbeat dance music, Latin music, African drums. Crank up the volume and dance until you sweat. Run, run as fast and as far as you can until your lungs feel as though they could explode. Sing at the top of your voice. Movement creates fire. Move your body, shake all over. Inhale scents of orange, cinnamon, lemon, peppermint. Burn natural candles with these scents, or use aromatherapy oils. Plan an adventure, or host a fiesta. Think about fire.

If your passion is too high, wear blue and lavender. Burn blue and light lavender candles daily. Paint a wall or an entire room in your house blue, lavender, or light pink. Eat calming foods, such as soft puddings, chocolate, homemade creamy soups, soft sweet fruits such as bananas, and roasted root vegetables. Listen to soothing music, soft classical tunes, wind chimes, nature sounds, flute, or harp. Do Yoga or engage in deep rhythmic breathing, or both. Lie down and meditate on nature. Inhale the scents of lavender, neroli, and sandalwood. Burn natural candles with these scents or use aromatherapy. Plan quiet evenings at home, warm baths, and restful activities.

PLEIADIAN KEY

THE ARTIST, CREATIVE SOURCE, CREATIVITY, UNIVERSAL CONNECTION, STAR ENERGY

Description

Two triangles connected, with the right one black or dark, and the left white or clear.

Origin

Pleiadian Key comes to us from the stars. As the symbol on Glyph implies, it serves a dual purpose as explained in the Interpretation. It is the most multi-faceted and complicated of all the Glyphs, because of its dual nature, and multiple meanings.

I will share an amusing story about how this symbol became a part of the Anam Glyphs. For an entire moon phase, I woke up every morning with the symbol fixed in my mind. It was familiar to me, but I did not know from where. I originally thought it was one of several glyphs gifted to me by Goddesses, its strange shape wrought by Great Mother Genesis herself. I asked my house squirrel to sketch it for me. Then one day, I streamed the Earth series Star Trek on my Crystal Interface, and upon seeing the characters in their Star Fleet uniforms, I broke into guffaws. Although not an exact replica, Pleiadian Key certainly resembles the Star Trek Starfleet Insignia! Yes. The

Goddesses gave this symbol to me through my subconscious after I'd binge watched the first two seasons of Captain Kirk and his crew wearing it. Nonetheless, although I unconsciously pulled Pleiadian Key from Hu Man pop culture, its significance is not in the least frivolous.

Interpretation

If you receive Pleiadian Key you are most likely an artist, or you are being put on notice that now is the time to cultivate your natural artistic instincts and talents. Most artists know that their inspiration, their muse, comes from a universal creative source. This Glyph unlocks our innate creative ability. Musicians, painters, sculptors, ceramicists, poets, novelists, dancers, great chefs, architects, performers, directors, designers, story tellers, inventors and creative thinkers who solve problems uniquely are all artists. You are among them.

Put Pleiadian Key in the place where you create, where you paint, or write, or think. When wishing to expand their repertoire or improve their technique, musicians can hold the key to their instruments, and singers can hold the key to their throats as they visualize their instruments, and vocal cords vibrating in tune with the music of the Universe. When an artist feels blocked, calling upon the energy of Pleiadian Key, which points toward the direction of the stars from where our creative energy originations, can serve as a reconnection between the heart and mind of the artist, and the infinite creative source which allows every artist to tap into a never ending abundance of creative ideas.

The second purpose of this Glyph is more universal in nature. Some say that we all seeded from the Sirius star system. Those from this system are the peaceful ones among us fully aware of our inner God/Goddess source. Others say the Pleiadian star system is where we originated, and that the most passionate artists, greatest thinkers, and builders among us are Pleiadians. However, according to some, Pleiadians were also a warring species who, once seeded on our planet, sought to dominate and subjugate the Sirius species. If you notice, this Glyph has two halves put together creating the complete symbol. The reason for this is to tell you that we are all part of the greater whole. Had we called this Glyph the Sirius Key instead of the Pleiadian Key, or something all together different, it would not matter. There is no "good" species or "bad" species, there just "is." We are all part of the same tribe. We come from the Pleiades and Sirius tribes, or Rendaz, or of Heaven, or God, or Mother Genesis, whatever your heart tells you. No matter what we call ourselves we are together, and together we are whole.

You may be feeling disconnected from others, from nature, from your very source. When Pleiadian Key makes an appearance, it is to remind us that we are creative beings who are part of each other, and we are all part of the Universe. The Key serves to unlock our creative nature, releasing the most profound secret of the Universe—our oneness with everything. We are connected to every star. We are connected to each planet in our Universe. We are connected to every single living being on our planets. From the largest mammal to the tiniest microbe, our connection to the great "all" is as real as the connection of our head to our bodies, or each finger to each of our hands. If you sometimes feel disconnected, Pleiadian Key is here to tell you that you are always part of the infinite whole; you are never alone. You are an artist among a community of artists.

This Glyph reminds us that each star is a gift of light, bright and beautiful. And, each star is a mirror image of the even more brilliant light that our beautiful spirits reflect back into the Universe. We are each a magnificent, unique work of art.

Call upon the Pleiadian Key to help you open the door between you and your infinite source, the very energy that unites us all. When you see an evening sky populated with stars, look up and fill your heart with joy because you are truly part of those stars, and as long as the stars shine, you are part of their wisdom, artistic inspiration, and love. Acknowledge the stars and thank them for their beauty. As you are watching the stars, the stars are watching you in return.

If you are suffering from an artistic block, call upon Pleiadian Key to help you reconnect with your art. If you are thinking about learning an art, now is the time. You are an artist.

Exercise

Sit quietly in a chair—outside at night under a moonless sky is best—in a place where you can actually see the stars. If that is not possible because it is too cold, or overcast, or if you live in a city or colony where there is too much light to see the stars, sit in a darkened room of your abode and imagine billions of stars above you. Imagine you are holding the Pleiadian Key in your hand as you would a paintbrush or a pen.

Imagine a beam of golden light shooting out from the point of the key. You can direct that beam anywhere at will. Use it to connect all the stars you see in the sky, or in your imaginary sky, with one unbroken line. Then, direct the beam back down to Mother Earth or Rendaz. Imagine the light beam connecting our planets, and all life on Earth or Rendaz, including every being, with one unbroken stream of golden light. Once you are satisfied all is connected, direct the beam of golden light directly toward the center of your heart. Hold it there for a moment. Imagine that energy, love, and creative force is traveling from the stars along the unbroken beam, and seals the connection between the stars, the planet, all that live on our planets, and your heart.

Deeply feel that connection; it is real. Then take Pleiadian Key and turn it clockwise three times to lock in that connection between you and the Great All. Put the key away somewhere safe, perhaps you will store it in a place where you keep your most valuable artists supplies, perhaps in a box made of light you hide among the stars. Know that the next time you feel disconnected, or blocked as an artist, you can easily reach out with your hand to retrieve the box, and the key will be there for you so that you can reconnect once again.

RAM

DESTROYER OF OBSTACLES, PHYSICAL AND EMOTIONAL ENERGY, STRENGTH

Description

The symbol of Ram is a U with spiral "horns" on each end, so as to look like a stylized image of a ram facing you.

Origin

The ram: tenacious, strong, with horns mighty enough to break down brick walls. Peggy A. says for years, whenever she found herself blocked, she imagined a spirit ram battering through all of the obstacles before her, allowing for free flow and progress. Peggy A. suggested we include Ram among the family of Glyphs, and I concur that it's a symbol we all need from time-to-time. Behold the ram's vitality, great force, and power to boost energy and destroy obstacles.

Interpretation

When this Glyph appears in your life, it is because you are in need of his energy. Call upon Ram to unblock your power and destroy obstacles to your progress or your life's work.

Ram is good medicine for anyone feeling weak, either because of a physical illness or injury, or because of emotional exhaustion. Use this symbol to knock down the obstacles that create weakness or frailty in your life. Ram is your strongest ally in helping you to overcome adversity of all kinds that drains your energy. Ram says he'll take care of things for you so that you can most certainly enjoy restored energy.

If you are overburdened, over stressed, or just tired, now is the time to invoke Ram. If you have recently suffered an emotional or physical trauma, or feel that you are faced with so many obstacles you find it difficult to progress, or even get up some days, or if you are undergoing a major life change that exhausts you, and depletes your energy, now is the time to invoke Ram. With this Glyph in your life, you are indeed on the road to mental, emotional, spiritual, or physical strength.

[When suffering from low energy, also look to Pelé Fire, and Greenleaf. Ram, Greenleaf and Pelé Fire are in close alliance to manifest energy, and for healing.]

Exercise

During times when you feel your energy has abandoned you, and your strength wanes for any reason, sit for a minute. Hold an image of Ram in your mind, and visualize the symbol knocking down your pile of obstacles for you with his huge curved horns. Over and over again, he butts his powerful head and horns against all of your obstacles, breaking them into bits. Then he stomps them into powder with his powerful hooves. Once all of your obstacles are smashed and rendered into useless powder, Ram faces you and looks directly into your face with his big brown eyes—he is directing his heart-energy to you. He gives you all the abundant strength and energy you need to overcome any stress in your life, enabling you to bear any burden, and to accomplish your goals. As you sense Ram's energy entering you, you begin to feel revitalized, energized. In your mind, walk to Ram.

Pull your fingers or paws though his thick wool. Take a moment to scratch Ram on his chin and head between his horns. He leans into you affectionately. Thank Ram for helping you. Pull an apple or carrot from your pocket and offer it to him. He takes it from your hand and walks back to an open green pasture and lies down beneath the shade of an ancient oak to enjoy his treat. Know that everything is going to be okay, and you are funded with the energy to accomplish anything, Ram has destroyed the obstacles to your success, and has helped clear the path for healing and achieving.

REST TIME

REST, INTROSPECTION, SLOWING DOWN, SLEEP, SELF-NURTURING

Description
Rest Time is represented by a straight horizontal line

Origin

In the Runic tradition, the symbol Isa (meaning "ice") means halt, immobility or "freeze in place." It also represents self-control, focus, and ego. Isa is symbolized by a straight vertical line.

Although Rest Time is also symbolized as a straight line, the line is horizontal rather than vertical, and represents a figure in repose. We included Rest Time because so many of us are in desperate need of rest, rejuvenation, and quiet time to think or nurture ourselves.

Interpretation

When Rest Time appears, it is time to slow your pace and reflect. This is the time for you to step away from your current plans and reflect on your direction. This is not the best time to embark on a new venture.

If you are in a hurry to get somewhere in your life, Rest Time says, "This is not the time to press on." You may be in need of more sleep, or more downtime. It's important to take a well deserved and much needed time-out. Look to the message of the Self Love Glyph. Are you nurturing yourself at all these days? Are you adequately caring for yourself? You must love yourself enough to get the rest your body, mind and soul needs and deserves. It is in times of rest and quiet that we open ourselves more fully to experiencing and developing ourselves. If we are overworked, or stressed out all the time, overextended, noisy, or in a rush, we cannot move forward. Without proper rest, we become less and less able to live a life of fulfillment. It is only during times of rest that we can be introspective. Rest Time tells you that you would be well served to slow down enough to look within and explore your inner landscape, because there is something important within for you to see, but you cannot see it if you are too busy to look. By the way, if you are thinking about a change, or a start-up to a new business, hold off. When this Glyph appears, it's not generally a good time to start anything new, or to make any significant changes.

Rest your busy mind. Be mindful of your constant internal chatter. Ask your monkey brain to quiet itself for a little while. Remove yourself from your troubles or your work to reflect on your life. Rest your vocal cords and your mouth. Be silent and listen to the world. Retire to your sleeping pillow an hour earlier, or sleep an hour later. Take a break from your schedule for an hour, a day, or longer with the intent of resting.

Even though you may feel you are too busy to slow down, you must. Rest Time cautions you that if you do not take a deliberate step back and relax when you need to, you could create for yourself some undesirable consequence, such as an illness, an accident, a state of emotional exhaustion, or a leg or foot injury. If you sustain an injury severe enough that you either cannot walk, or have trouble walking, such as a broken leg or torn tendon, it is a sure sign for you to slow down and rest. If you do not slow down, you may make a mistake that can result in pain for yourself or someone else. Rest is what we all need to rejuvenate ourselves physically and mentally, and to nourish our souls.

Exercise

Literally, take a day off from your work or daily routine. If you cannot manage a way to do that, take a half day. Find a way, any way, to be by yourself away from everyone and everything to read a book, write in your journal, and to sleep. If at all possible, spend time in the natural world. Align yourself with the slow rhythm of nature, the sound of a rambling brook, the music of a bird, and the breeze.

If you cannot be in nature, then create a natural world for yourself. Create a space in a room of your abode with green living plants, cut flowers, pine cones, rocks, crystals, green candles, pieces of drift wood, or shells. Stream music of nature sounds, the forest or the ocean, or of birdsong, temple bells, or wind chimes. If you do not have such music, now is the time to buy some. Sit within your created natural world, or the actual outdoors, and listen carefully to the sounds. Watch clouds drifting over the sky. If it is not feasible to be outside, also viewing clouds from your mind's eye is fine. Listen to the rain pattering, or the wind blowing, or the waves of the sea licking the shoreline. Watch how the sunlight shifts, alternately touching the trees, the rocks, and the ground. Feel the sun, breeze, cooling rain, or snow flakes, against your skin, fur, scales, feathers or hide, whatever covers your body. You can also sit in a bathtub, a river, or a hot tub and attune yourself to the natural world, surrounded by your green candles, green plants, flowers, and stones.

Practice a day of being SLOW. Deliberately walk slowly, chew your food slowly one bite at a time, speak slowly, breathe in and out slowly. Carry the Rest Time Glyph with you in your pocket, or in your wing, paw, or robes. Touch it often to remind yourself to slow down and rest.

ROYAL ELK

THE LEADER, SEXUAL POTENCY, POWER, FOREST ENERGY, MALE ENERGY, THE GREEN MAN

Description

Royal elk is represented by a single antler with eight prongs.

Origin

The Royal Elk wears eight points on his antlers, a sign of strength and longevity. The points on the Royal Elk's rack are also the symbol for infinity. Only the bull elk in the wild that has managed to survive the harsh elements, disease, the hunter's bow or bullet, and the attack of the mountain lion will live long enough to achieve royal status.

In the western Earth world, the Royal Elk, along with the bear, the moose and the mountain lion, shares the rank of King of the Forest. The vibration for the number eight is one of prosperity and leadership.

Interpretation

When called upon, you can be a great leader. Receiving this glyph is a symbol of your own personal power. Those with Royal Elk energy are powerful, passionate, magical people by nature.

Conversely, some people with Royal Elk energy need to awaken their inner power and passion. Either way, those who carry Royal Elk energy with them are cautioned to remind themselves from time-to-time to temper their pride. In spite of their natural power, or perhaps because of it, they need to remain humble. The most commanding and effective leaders are always passionate, and strong, but never prideful.

Royal Elk funds you with the ability to achieve great things, to lead others, and to overcome adversity. If you are making plans, and are not sure if this is the right time to move ahead with them, Royal Elk says "Yes. Go forward! You have a good chance at success."

Royal elk is a sexual being, and when in rut, becomes incredibly potent. The piercing bugle of the elk during rutting season can be heard for dozens of miles throughout the forest. Weighing in at over 1,200 lbs, with his impressive rack of antlers, the Royal Elk is indeed a force to be reckoned with. Green Man, the Lord of the Forest, is depicted wearing either stag or elk antlers on his head. To some, the Royal Elk *IS* the Green Man in his most basic, animalistic form because he, like the Green Man, is a magical being of the natural green realms that cross between the forests of our world and the forests in the world of the unseen.

Royal Elk comes into your life to help you to awaken your power, your leadership ability, or your sexual vitality. He infuses you with his magical male energy. Whenever you are in need of primal male energy, or want a "power surge," call upon the magic of Royal

Note: When you receive Royal Elk, also take a look at Pelé Fire's message.

Exercise

Go somewhere where you can be alone and make some noise. Stand tall. Pretend you are Royal Elk in your primal forest, stepping proudly with your head held high. Your rack of antlers is magnificent. You have earned these because you live your life well.

Feel the weight of the antlers on your head. Move your head the way a Royal Elk does when bearing the weight of an eight-point rack. You are the ruler. Imagine you are stronger and more powerful than any other forest being. Your muscles are bulging and taut. Your back is strong. You are a passionate being. And, you are so wise and strong, and so absolutely magical, that you can face anything, survive anything, and be anything you desire. When you can fully see yourself as the Royal Elk, the leader, raise taller, stretch right up as far as you are able, and bugle loudly with all the strength and might you can muster. The male power of the Royal Elk is now your power.

SACRED TRIO

THE SPIRITUAL PERSON, HOLY TRINITY, SPIRITUALITY

Description

The Symbol of Sacred Trio, a Power Stone, is a stylized Number 3, resembling the "Om" or "Aum," and there are three dots, one to the top, one to the right side, and one integrated into the numeral three. Again, there is no exact way to create this symbol. Follow your heart.

Origin

This Glyph represents triple aspect of the soul, and when integrated, our triple aspect is the true essence of who we are. It's form is similar to the "Om" sign, The syllable "Om" or "Aum" is of paramount importance in Hinduism.

This symbol is sacred to the Hindus, and represents the "Brahman," omnipotent, omnipresent, the source of "all." Om represents the unmanifest (nirguna) and manifest (saguna) God or Goddess aspects.

Interpretation

When you receive this Glyph, it means you are known in some circle as an "old soul," on target to becoming a highly spiritually developed being. This Glyph represents triple aspect of our soul, and when integrated, our triple aspect is the true essence of who we are. When you receive Sacred Trio, the most powerful Gods and Goddesses guide you. You are called upon to pray or meditate on the triple aspects of your spirituality, to work on integrating all facets of your being through your connection with them, and with those special being who exist on the physical plane.

Additionally, Sacred Trio calls upon you to form alliances with those who will help you to remain grounded, and asks that you permit others to instruct you. You will do well to learn from the experience of those who are here to support your soul's accelerated growth.

When I need grounding, I call upon Samuel S. Goodwings, the most down–to-planet being I know. He reminds me, during those times when my head is in the clouds, to keep all four of my feet on the ground lest I float away.

When you receive the Sacred Trio express yourself through speaking, writing, teaching or performing for the purpose of enlightening others rather than entertaining, and you may already be doing these things. Soul expression is your keynote, and you can behold the joy of living with expression in its many forms. However, those among us who have evolved to the point where you are now, often struggle the most with the Hu Man or Rendazian experience. Sometimes you may feel trapped in this material world, and are frustrated. As a result, you may act in a manner contrary to your evolving spiritual nature. When you receive Sacred Trio, know that unseen powers are assisting you on your journey. Even though life may present some interesting challenges to you, all your experiences are a part of your evolution, and you indeed walk among the most fortunate and blessed among us.

For you, it's especially important to remain humble. Sacred Trio asks that you be accepting and loving of others exactly where they are at this point in their evolvement. Remember that all beings are perfect expressions of the divine, all of us equal on this plane of existence. Open your heart. Ground yourself. Be intent on acquiring the greater understanding you require to progress and to fully realize all the magnificent aspects of the true you.

Exercise

Commit to recognizing the divinity within yourself and each being you meet today. See all individuals as progressing along their paths differently, at different rates of speed within their own timing, operating under their own perfect agreement with the Universe. See everyone today as perfect and holy.

Stand in front of a mirror and look directly into your own eyes. Proclaim to yourself: "I am a perfect expression of the Divine. I am truly a magnificent, and highly evolved spiritual being, whole and complete. I am also a common being. I acknowledge I have much to teach others, and as much to learn from them in return. I am grateful for my mundane experience, and for all the incredible teachers on this physical plane." Wear hematite, or carry a hematite stone with you, to help keep you grounded and centered, and to assist you with integrating your soul's different aspects.

SEAGULL

FREEDOM

Description

The Seagull glyph is represented by a line with two stylized wings to represent a bird. As part of the symbol, are choppy ocean waves the bird skims in flight.

Origin

The one word universally symbolic of any bird is "freedom." However, the seagull is very special because of all the water birds, the seagull is not only a master of the skies, but is also one of the birds most commonly associated with the ocean. Who has been near an ocean and not heard the distinct cry of the seagull? And when hearing a seagull, who is not reminded of a sandy beach, recalled the rich briny smell of an ocean, or heard in our mind the crashing of waves against powerful boulders?

The seagull serves as the link between the endless sky under which we all live, and our planets immense oceans. Water is an ancient symbol of emotions, hidden spirituality and our deepest psychic ability. Water represents our instincts, our wisdom, our ability to transmute experience into knowledge. The ocean, with its unfathomable depths and mysteries, is the center of many of our most powerful universal myths, and is also the most powerful of all water symbols. Air and sky represent intellect, inspiration, and our ability to be completely open to, and conscious of, our spiritual nature as it manifests itself within our human intelligence.

Interpretation

Seagull says to us, "Yes, we are free to be ourselves, intellectually, spiritually, and emotionally." The seagull will help you to freely understand and express yourself, while at the same time assisting you to develop and nurture extraordinary abilities of perception and intuition. The seagull is here to teach you that your heart and head are most powerful when they work together. Seagull is here to help you to safely dive into the mysterious depths of your emotional and spiritual life, while simultaneously allowing you to soar freely into your intellect, opening yourself to inspired thought and idea.

When you are beginning any new venture, particularly a new business or some kind of financial endeavor, or are starting out on a new life's adventure, keep the seagull nearby. If at all possible, visit the ocean, walk on a sandy beach barefooted, and listen for the song of the seagull. When you feel trapped or stuck, are seeking freedom, and feel emotionally or spiritually bound, call on seagull energy.

Exercise

If you are feeling imprisoned within in your personal circumstances and crave freedom, bring an image into your mind of the seagull flying over the waves of an ocean. Hold that image for a while until you begin to create a sense of harmony between your heart and mind. This will take practice. However, over time, with daily use of this exercise, you could enjoy a new found freedom that is as immense as the sky and as deep as the ocean.

SELF LOVE

LOVING ONESELF, RECOGNIZING AND APPRECIATING ONE'S TRUE NATURE

Description

Self Love is represented by the figure of an androgynous Hu Man, with arms stretched up and over the head.

Origin

The figure of Self Love is familiar in Earthian Goddess and Dianic Wiccan cultures. Although our "Self Love" is androgynous, because males must love themselves, too, it is a recognizable goddess figure that people from both our worlds will recognize and identify with on a profound, or even deeply unconscious, level.

Interpretation

When the symbol of Self Love appears, it is because you have not been treating yourself kindly enough. Now is the time to recognize and appreciate your true nature, and to celebrate YOU. This is a time for self-appreciation, for acknowledging your own magnificence and perfection, for honoring the beauty and wisdom you were born with, and resides within you now. Too often we beat ourselves up. We reprimand ourselves for slip-ups, and punish ourselves for past mistakes. Even though we are kind and loving to others, we are terribly harsh and unloving to ourselves.

If you find yourself playing the "self blame game," feeling angry with yourself, or talking down to yourself, stop. Your heart is crying out to you because it is in desperate need of your respect, your kindness, and your love. When your self-talk is mean spirited, your thoughts about yourself are cruel or harsh, you put yourself down, or punish yourself by eating the wrong foods, or too much food, drinking too much alcohol, or numbing yourself with drugs, refusing to take the time to nurture yourself and your body, you disrespect who you are.

If you find you continually attract people who are mean to you, or if you have difficulty forming lasting, loving relationships, look to Self Love. In some cases, our lack of self-love is so powerful it serves to repel those people we seek to attract, and we are in danger of becoming lonely, bitter, depressed and dismal. If you are among those sad people, the good news is you can change that right now by committing to loving yourself completely and unconditionally.

Another important message Self Love has for you is that at times you must say "no." Part of loving the self is being able to set appropriate boundaries. If you honor yourself, you will not try to be all things to all people, or do everything others ask you to do. Self Love is here to remind you that you are a child of the Universe. You deserve to treat yourself with all the kindness and love you give to others. Notice that the Self Love Glyph is standing upright in a joyful stance hands raised overhead sensing and embracing the light of the self. The figure could be dancing, so joyful within its own self-love. Call this image to mind any time you find yourself being in the least bit impatient or unloving with yourself. The more often you bring Self Love into your life the more frequently you experience joy.

Exercise

Imitate the stance of Self-Love. If you are able to, stand in the posture of Self Love with your hands and arms lifted overhead. Feel the energy of your soul's light emanating from your crown chakra. Close your eyes, and say, "I can feel your beautiful light, [your name]. You are special and I love you." Say that several times out loud. Then, focus your energy on your heart while bringing to your mind an image of 'you hugging you.' As you do this, drop your arms down, hug yourself tightly, and say, "I love you, precious one. I honor, accept and love you [your name] exactly as you are." This may feel awkward at first because you may not be accustomed to showing love to yourself, or accepting love. Keep repeating the exercise until you sense a shift.

For me as a hippo, I have to imagine that I am Hu Man or some other ape, and I must know what I imagine is real. In that shifting moment of embracing ourselves, we are expressing deep love for who we are. Allow yourself to gratefully accept and fully experience the feelings of love. Move if you feel like it. Dance if you want to. Cry with joy if you feel like it. Continue the exercise, repeating the movements and the words until you feel like doing all of these things.

Plan something nice for yourself as a reward for being the magnificent person you are. Take a solitary walk in nature. Enjoy a long soothing bath by yourself. Get together with a good friend or loved one for a special day out. Get a massage. Take yourself on a date to an uplifting movie and dinner. Take a day off from your usual routine to read an enjoyable, inspiring book. Buy yourself a special gift. Make yourself a delicious meal and share it with another, or enjoy on your own, whatever feels best to you. Do something loving just for you.

SEQUOIA

THE ENVIRONMENTAL WARRIOR, ANCIENT WISDOM, ENVIRONMENTAL ISSUES

Description

Sequoia is represented by a stick with branches, a simple line drawing of a tree.

Origin

The Giant Sequoia is the wizened sentinel of the forest. Left alone, these trees live to be thousands of years old. Many of them alive today predate Hu Man Christianity, and can grow to be more than 300 feet high. Powerful and resilient, these trees survive lightening strikes, fires, earthquakes, all other manner of natural disasters, and sometimes, even when cut down, they regenerate themselves.

When walking through an old growth redwood forest one can sense the massive energy, great wisdom, and the spirituality alive within these trees. Whenever you see a Sequoia, whether in nature, in a photograph or movie, or whenever you receive the Sequoia Glyph, know that you have been offered a gift of spiritual strength, resilience, and wisdom. Some indigenous tribes of Earth Americas refer to trees as "standing people." Trees are alive and capable of feeling fear and pain, joy, and love in a way that transcends Hu Man understanding. On Rendaz, to harm a tree carries with it the same weight as murdering a Hu Man on Earth. Some of our old Rendazian trees actually speak, and all the old trees share wisdom. We've a council of Old Trees that help guide Rendazians.

Interpretation

When you receive Sequoia in a reading, it's a reminder to honor the spirit of these standing people who provide all creatures, including Hu Mans and Rendazians, with shelter, shade and protection. Trees that live together in a big forest are so powerful they actually affect climate and are vital to maintaining the natural balance of our planets.

Be as the Sequoia, still, steadfast, resilient, spiritually strong, wise and powerful. And, if you love and honor your brother/sister trees, and strive to protect them, you will be truly blessed because the trees will protect you in return. The Sequoia can renew your spiritual energy and provide you with inner wisdom beyond measure.

Sequoia means that you tasked with the divine undertaking of protecting, preserving and restoring our natural resources, including our waterways, our air, the forests, and our wildlife. Sequoia is aware of your caring heart, and is looking to you to be a steward of our natural world.

Exercise

When the Sequoia symbol appears in your life, you are given the message that you must undertake a meaningful role in preserving our worlds' natural resources. If possible, take a walk outside, sit under the trees and listen to what they tell you. Thank them for their wisdom.

If you cannot walk among the trees, go outside, no matter the climate, weather, or terrain, no matter if you live in the country, the desert, the suburbs, or in a small flat in a noisy city, walk outside for a moment. Imagine the sequoias, and thank them. Plant a sequoia seedling, if you can. Nurture it and honor it. And, while you're at it, join or donate to the environmental group of your choosing.

SPIRIT BRIDGE

MAGIC AND PASSAGES, BRIDGE BETWEEN THE SEEN AND UNSEEN WORLDS

Description

This glyph is represented by a line drawing of a bridge over water.

Origin

The bridge is an old symbol both on Earth and Rendaz for "crossing over" to discover something new, foreign, strange, or way to travel to a better place where the grass is greener. Bridges also symbolize death. Who among us has not heard of "crossing the rainbow bridge"?

In Earthian mythology, the bridge represents a pathway to paradise. The crossing of a bridge can mean a test of the soul's worthiness. Islam teaches about the "Bridge of Jehennam," or "Al Sarat," a bridge more thin than a single strand from a spider's web, with edges sharper than a sword's blade. At death, Hu Mans cross the bridge. The righteous are met on the other side by a white horse who spirits them to Heaven. The evil fall from the bridge into a pit of fire.

In the Japanese Shinto religion, has Ama-no-uki-hashi, a bridge that Hu Mans must cross to get into their version of paradise. This bridge, also known as The Floating Bridge of

Heaven, serves as the connection between the sky gods and Earth. The Incas believed that their heaven, Hana Pacha, can only be accessed by a bridge made of hair.

The Zoroastrians believe in the Bridge of Judgment or the Bridge of Separator, where every soul is evaluated after death. Those with good hearts are met by a beautiful maiden who escorts them to paradise. The evil are met by an ugly creature who makes the bridge increasingly narrow so that the wicked fall into a hellish pit. In the Norse tradition, the supernatural Heimdall guards the flame-covered Bilford Bridge that connects Midgard to Asgard. This bridge is depicted as a fiery rainbow. In some Indigenous American belief systems, Owl Woman guards the bridge to the afterlife. There are sacred bridges in Malay culture, in Persian culture, and bridges "to a better place" play roles in Rendazian culture, too. In the Wayflower District of Rendaz where I was born and live still, we have the myth of the invisible Kwa Bridge. It is said that once very Cool Season (your Earth Winter) when both moons are full, the bridge over the Kwa River becomes visible to Believers. It is said if you cross it just before it disappears in to the mist, you will meet The Great Goddess Genesis, and she will give you a blessing to take back. It is fitting that a bridge would be represented among the Glyphs.

Interpretation

When you receive this Glyph, you are a magical person already in communion with your mystical self. You already know that we live in a magical universe and our possibilities are limitless. Or, perhaps, contrarily, you have lost your connection with magic, and you are meant to reconnect with the elemental world.

Spirit Bridge invites you to cross over to the unseen dimension for a while. On Rendaz, fairies, unicorns, mermaids, leprechauns, Sasquatch, and all other manner of mythical beasts and magical beings do indeed exist, as do the spirits and ghosts of loved ones who have crossed over. However, on Earth these beings and spirits may have gone extinct with the meteor, or perhaps live in a parallel world to yours, unseen by most who live on this side of the bridge. As children, Hu Mans readily accept the existence of magic. Children of Earth often see spirit beings, fairies, ghosts of those who have passed on, and magical lights, which they no longer are able to perceive once they have reached the age of seven or so, the age when they begin to listen to what adults tell them. Once that happens, the "veil of disillusionment" descends, obscuring the possibility that magic exists, sadly for most, *forever*.

Spirit Bridge connects worlds. The possibility this Glyph offers is that this bridge enables us to not only see, but also actually interact with sprites, fairy folk, and other magical creatures from Hu Man mythology, and to commune with those who have passed on. Spirit Bridge has powerful magic to make the unseen seen, the unheard heard, the unfelt felt, the invisible visible.

If you are a magical being engaged in your own sense of mysterious power, then Spirit Bridge asks you to lead others over the bridge. If you have lost your sense of wonder and magic, and need to reconnect with the elemental world, or wish to visit with someone who has passed on, use the exercise below to find out how to cross the bridge for a little visit. Here's the best part, once you have even once crossed the bridge and have returned, you may begin to notice, sense, hear or see things that you did not before. What about that *little something* out of the corner of your eye that is not there when you turn to face it? What about the rustle of a wing when nothing has flown by, or the sensation that something or someone has gently touched your shoulder? Or, what of that soft whispering that sounds a little bit like a voice? When you are receptive, you may actually see a spirit being in its full glory. Or, you may sit a while and visit with an ancestor, or a friend who has crossed over. Yes, they can most certainly be *real*, and they can cross the bridge to visit us, just as we cross the bridge to visit them.

Another meaning attached to the bridge is passage to the other side. In rare cases, Spirit Bridge may be telling you that someone you care for is ready to cross the bridge, meaning they will soon leave this existence and travel to another plane, either physically (as in to portend a death of the body), or metaphorically. Sometimes it means that aspects of a person "dies" allowing for a rebirth, a new start.

And, of course, Spirit Bridge can also herald a message from the other realms, perhaps from a loved one who has passed into the arms of the Goddess.

Exercise

To cross the Spirit Bridge, sit still and close your eyes. Imagine what the bridge is made from, stone, wood, blue light, gold? Imagine its color, white, tan, ebony, purple, silver? Is it covered with moss, or diamonds? Are there carvings or decorations on the bridge? Is the bridge covered with flowers, vines of English ivy, or moss, or nothing at all? Is it a big bridge or a small footbridge? See what it straddles—a river, a stream, a gorge, a valley, a desert, a canyon, a bottomless purple breech in the earth? See the world you are in now, and then face the bridge. Know that once you cross it, you will be stepping into a parallel existence, new and ancient at the same time. Remove your shoes, if you wear them, and take a step on the bridge in your bare feet. What does the bridge feel like? Is it warm or cool on your feet, rough or smooth? Walk one step at a time toward a distant glow on the other side.

Once you are halfway across the bridge, a glimpse of what is on the other side comes into view. As you approach nearer the other side, what do you see there? An ancient old growth forest shrouded in fog? An endless white sand beach on the shores of a deep azure ocean? A sunny meadow covered in a million wildflowers? A brilliant colored desert with thousands of cacti in bloom? Red canyons? Soaring rock formations with hundreds of striations in purple and tan covered with ancient petroglyphs? A deserted tropical island? A deep cave in a magical mountain? Is there a pond, lichen covered boulders, a path, a waterfall, a hundred waterfalls? What do you smell? Hyacinth in bloom? The briny ocean? Savory stew cooking in a kettle? What do you hear? The rush of water? Birdsong? Music? Bells? The soft flapping of tiny wings? Where are you? Ireland? The United States? Rendaz? Mesopotamia? Africa? Atlantis? Avalon? Lemuria? The Garden of Eden?

Once you know where you are, connect with your heart space and ask to meet your magical being. Who is it that you want to see, speak with, and interact with, perhaps a long-deceased relative, a talking unicorn, a fairy queen, a mermaid or merman, Sasquatch, the Goddess Diana, Pan, the Green Man? Or perhaps you want to communicate with a loved one who has passed into the arms of the Goddess? If what appears to you is a magical being, what does he or she look like to you—short, tall? What kind of features does this person or being have? What clothes are they wearing, or are they unclothed? How long is their hair, or do they even have hair? Is this being male or female? Is anyone with them, or did they come to you alone? If others are with them, who are they?

As the person or magical being approaches you, greet them in the way you feel is best with a nod, a bow, a smile, a hug, or a word. Then wait for them to respond. How do they greet you? Do they have a name? If so, what is their name? What does the person or being say to you? The person or magical being wants to give you something, or tell you something important, what is it? Sit with them for a while, and talk. What do you talk about? Do you share food or drink? Once you feel that your conversation is complete, say your goodbyes. You can choose to meet another person or magical being, or several, or many. You may stay as long as you like. You are safe and welcomed on this side of the bridge. When you feel your visit is complete, and you are ready to return home, express your gratitude for the hospitality of your hosts, and then walk over the bridge back home. Breathe in deeply, once you have returned, sense your surroundings back on this side of the bridge. When you are ready, open your eyes and notice your feelings. You may cross the bridge at any time you want to visit the other world, any time at all.

STONE WHEEL

MOVEMENT, ADVANCEMENT, FORWARD MOTION, NEW DWELLING PLACES

Description

Stone Wheel is represented by a drawing of a stone age wheel with a hole in the middle, not unlike a fat donut made of granite.

Origin

This symbol represents the ancient wheel, which in ancient Earthian times was used to transport massive loads as well as to crush grain, and was put to many other useful purposes. In the more modern world, the wheel might be used to turn the hands of a clock, to enable transportation, and to run all manner of machinery. Without the wheel, there would be no automobiles or trains. Even airplanes and ocean liners depend upon wheels. Beyond being the archetypal symbol of progress, the wheel represents forward movement, and gives those who receive the wheel's energy the ability to literally and figuratively transport themselves.

Interpretation

When the Stone Wheel appears in your life, you are on notice that you have the capability to move forward, freeing yourself from confinement, easily bearing any load you must carry, and you are provided with the means to do anything you choose. The shape of the wheel is round, meaning there is no ending, no beginning. Therefore, as of this moment forward, know your ability to move forward is limitless and never ending. When you recognize the wheel anywhere, rejoice because it gives you a message that you are on the right track, and you are indeed making progress.

Since the wheel also symbolizes physical transportation and movement, be on the lookout for opportunities to travel, or for a move to a new dwelling place, or a move to a new job. But, even if your movement is not literal or physical, receiving Stone Wheel means you are now rolling into a new phase of your life. You are progressing.

Exercise

Recline on a couch, bed, or on your sleeping pillows. Close your eyes and think about how you want to move on from some phase of your life, but you are stuck. Are you unable to advance forward in your career, or with your relationships, or in a particular project, or in your personal development? Identify where your life is at a standstill. Notice in your body where you feel the emotion of being held down or held back. Is it in your stomach, neck, back, your head? Wherever there is a sensation of tightness or pain, or pressure that is where your body is holding onto those stuck feelings.

Close your eyes. Imagine your body is on the ground with powerful glue trapping you there. You cannot get up. You cannot move in any direction. You can move your head a little to side-to-side. You can open and close your eyes, but that is all you can move. You feel like you weigh a million pounds. In the distance, you hear a sound like footsteps crunching on gravel. Something or someone is moving in your direction. It is Stone Wheel coming to pull you out of the glue. Stone Wheel appears to you in his Hu Man form, a tall man, powerfully built with snow-white hair to his waist bound in two thick braids. He is thousands of years old, but his face is unlined. His eyes are black. His skin is the color of burnished copper. He has a long aquiline nose and a strong chin. His lips are thin.

Although you sense that he is a kind elder he does not smile because he is on an important mission. His is here to "free you" and help you move forward. This is very serious business for Stone Wheel. He wears blue jeans but is barefooted, and his chest is bare. He has large hands but they are gentle, and his fingers are long and delicate. On his back between his shoulder blades is a tattoo of a stone wheel. He turns his back to you and raises his hands to the air. You open your eyes and watch. You see the stone wheel tattoo. He raises his head to the sky and sings a prayer in a language you do not understand. After a few minutes, the stone wheel on his back glows with a pale light, and then spins slowly. The man ceases his prayer, lowers his head, drops his hands, and turns toward you. He stands over your body as you remain stuck fast to the ground, face-up looking at him. You are not afraid. He takes his left hand and places it on his heart. He takes his right hand and suspends it palm down over the place in your body where you feel the emotion of being stuck. A warm beam of light comes through the center of the palm of his hand and penetrates that stuck place within you. You feel comforting warmth, a loosening, and then a release. You hear a low humming coming from the light emanating from Stone Wheel's hand. After a bit, you feel the glue that has held you in place for so long begin to soften. Within a few minutes, you can freely move your arms, your head, and your legs.

The light and humming from the man's hand fades. With both hands, he reaches down to you and pulls you to your feet. The glue has vanished completely. It's as though it was never holding you in place. He stands in front of you, and looks directly into your eyes. He says to you "My sister/brother, you are now free to move forward in your life. You may go anywhere you choose." You know that what he says is true. You are no longer stuck. You thank him. He smiles, turns into a white raven and flies into the sky higher and higher until you can no longer see him.

TRICKY BOY

THE TRICKSTER, BREAKING THROUGH ILLUSION, HUMOR, LAUGHING AT ONE'S FOIBLES

Description

Tricky Boy is represented by a Hu Man like face without a nose, two black holes for eyes, and a broad, crooked smile. He wears a silly hat with a short brim.

Origin

In some cultures, Tricky Boy is known as Loki, Coyote, The Fool, Snake, The Clown, and in Rendazian culture, Jackalope.

This Glyph represents the imp that causes unexplained electrical problems in your house or automobile. He is the one who makes you stub your toe on the rock you didn't see. He will cause your computer to go wacky for no apparent reason, or your cell phone, or make your Crystal Interface drop one call after another at the most inconvenient time.

Tricky Boy pastes the toilet tissue to the bottom of your shoe as you leave the restroom of an upscale restaurant, and causes the piece of spinach to lodge in your front teeth at the time you most want to make a favorable impression. He is the great mastermind behind the "flukes" of our life. He does these things to teach us important lessons, or to make us stop where we are and laugh at our current situation. When you become frustrated or even very angry over these annoying things that just seem to happen all on their own for no logical reason, Tricky Boy rolls on the floor with laughter.

Interpretation

Ha, ha! Tricky Boy is here, you lucky person. When Tricky Boy comes into your life, he is here to tell you a few things, and you better listen carefully or the joke is on you!

Tricky Boy appears in your life to smash your illusions. If you allow him to, Tricky Boy will crack your façade so that your real self shines through. He knows that as your authentic self, you might even have a little more fun. Because he wants you to have a better life, Tricky Boy doesn't pull any punches. "When I come around, the jig is up," he says. Tricky Boy always tells it like it is! People either love or hate Tricky Boy. I know Peggy A. Wheeler cringes when Tricky Boy appears in her readings. I find that humorous!

This Glyph makes an appearance now and again to help us burst through our self-illusions so that we may live a more purposeful and joyful life, or to teach us an important lesson. "Breaking away from our self-created illusions need not be difficult," says Tricky Boy, "but we do have to be willing to leave behind all the deception and stinky false stuff we have accumulated over our lifetime to protect our need to be right, or that we cling to so we can justify our actions or words when they hurt others." Tricky Boys says, "To be happy, we have to be willing to give up our stories. Great Flaming Fritters, we all love our stories!" says Tricky Boy. "We even like to believe our stories are actually real. Aren't beings funny that way?" In our stories, we have invented a whole cast of characters including lots of villains and heroes, and victims. Tricky Boy tells us we often like to play the role of victim in our story because it wins us attention or sympathy, and we get to be "right" and someone else "wrong." If someone else is wrong, we don't have to be responsible, do we?

Tricky Boy knows once we stop making up stories about our life, and quit re-running our stories over and over again in our mind's movie theater, we can live in joy. Until then we choose suffering over happiness every time. Our stories are usually grand, epic, tragic dramas which culminate in tear-jerking, miserable, angst-filled endings, sometimes with one or more of the main characters perpetrating some unforgivable life damaging wrong against the hero (us), or hurting then abandoning the victim protagonist. Rarely do we ever give our life story a happy ending.

"Ha, ha" says Tricky Boy, "I laugh at you wannabe directors and actors in your own pretend stories, because even if you are so very good at directing and acting that you believe in your own silly made-up stuff. Tricky Boy knows better. I get the big joke! Do you? Ha! Ha!"

Oh, and another thing, besides too often fooling yourself, Tricky Boy says you take yourself too seriously. When you see Tricky Boy you are meant to laugh a little more. See the irony and the humor in life. Watch a funny movie. Read a funny book. Turn your work into play, and your play into ecstasy. You may have serious and important work to do, and may be saddled with many responsibilities, but your daily life need not be filled with drama, suffering, pain, sadness or seriousness. Re-write the script of your life. Turn your life's story into a comedy, or great romance, or a grand adventure instead of a tragedy. How about having fun for a change? Tricky Boy's message is that life is meant to be a hoot and a half, filled with one hysterical, sidesplitting guffaw after another.

Once on Rendaz I had a run-in with an evil coyote, Belinda. I suspected her of criminal activity. She'd left with her pack for an evening howl, but I arrive later than I should have. I sneaked into her abode to break into her Wise Woman Diary to find evidence for Sergeant Saturday so he'd have just cause to arrest her. After a good many attempts, I finally guessed her password to her Crystal Interface. I discovered her written confession, exactly what I needed, but just as I was about to project the file to Sergeant Saturday, her Crystal Interface froze and the file hung suspended on the screen. Try as I might, I could not project it. It was right then I heard Belinda turn the key in her lock. Had she not dropped her key, had to paw the ground to find it, and secure it back into her teeth so she could turn the lock, she would have caught me in her abode on her Crystal Interface.

The instant she retrieved her key, and turned the latch to open the door, the file vanished with a pop, and the message "file projected successfully," appeared. I barely had time to back out of the rear flap of her abode before she stepped in. I knew Tricky Boy was at work to remind me to use more caution, and in the doing, I have no doubt the little scoundrel got a good laugh at my expense.

Exercise

Practice this as often as possible: Pay attention. Quit taking yourself so seriously. Get over yourself, and go play!

TWENTYNINE

THE HUMANITARIAN, COMPASSIONATE PEACEMAKER

29

Description

The Glyph Twentynine is simply the number 29.

Origin

This Glyph's symbol originates from Earthian Numerology. The number two, linked to the Tarot's 'The High Priestess,' signifies among other things, the Peacemaker. Furthermore, two is associated with 'The All Knowing.'

The number nine, related to the Tarot's 'The Hermit' signifies, among other things, 'Global Awareness' and is helpful, compassionate, and charitable. Nine is associated with 'the humanitarian.'

Two plus Nine equals Eleven, a master number in numerology, linked to the Tarot's 'Justice,' and is known to be 'The Most Intuitive.' Eleven, signifies, among other things, dynamism, passion, capability, and serves as a link between dark and light, mortality and immortality, ignorance and enlightenment.

Interpretation

"Life's most persistent and urgent question is, 'What are you doing for others?'"

— Martin Luther King Jr.

Every single one of us has our own unique path but the core of our greater purpose is always service to others. When you receive Twentynine, it is because you are a compassionate, giving human being, and you are being celebrated for your loving heart. The spirit of this Glyph recognizes your service, and calls you to action by asking you to work with others to further your cause of serving humanity. Receiving this Glyph is your assurance that you have all the ability, qualifications, skill, time, and the great compassion you need to be a true humanitarian. In your heart of hearts, you must come to know that the difference you might make in the world cannot be made by another.

As a compassionate humanitarian, Twentynine asks you to help others to realize their own humanitarian calling, as well. With all the work that needs to be done on our planets, I am astonished to hear of people who retire, and then waste the remainder of their lives waiting to die, or simply indulging in idle pleasures that after a short while leave one empty. How many times have you heard someone say, "I can never retire because I wouldn't know what to do with my time?" Twentynine's response is "How about working for Habitat for Humanity, Greenpeace, Sierra Club, Defenders of Wildlife, raising money for The Butterfly Council, or donating hours or money to a battered women's shelter, a soup kitchen, or a peace organization?"

People who do not use their talents to help others, and have nothing constructive to do with their time when they are not being paid to work, are those who think only of themselves.

Opportunities abound for everyone to be in service to others, to do meaningful work, and sometimes others may need your assistance to recognize and grasp those opportunities.

You are a caring and loving person who strives always to give as much, or more, as you receive. You indeed have a generous soul. When Twentynine appears, it is a message that the Universe is grateful for what you do, and is looking to you to further use your talents, resources and knowledge in even greater service to others. Call on Twentynine to help you continue to cultivate and strengthen your compassion, or when you wish to help others to do the same. The joy you will receive from serving is 10,000 times that of being served.

Exercise

A good daily practice for one who wishes to cultivate their humanitarian spirit is the "Wishing Bowl" meditation. Find a small bowl, or make one. Write or etch the number 29 into the bowl. You may also place a small stone, a crystal, a feather, something from the natural world that has meaning for you into the bowl. However, just the number 29 will do. As you gaze into the bowl, with all the love and light you can pull forth into your lungs, breathe a wish into it for someone else. The one rule is the wish you make cannot be a wish for yourself or that knowingly benefits you. In return for your selfless wishes, you will be blessed in ways you cannot even imagine.

WATERBUG

JOY, PLAYFULNESS, EASE, BALANCE

Description

Waterbug is represented by a straight line with two sets of legs, one set forward, the other facing the back.

Origin

Examine the Waterbug Glyph and notice how it is designed to move in any direction with ease, gliding over the surface of the water effortlessly, lightly, and quickly.

Water represents important spiritual aspects of life's experience, but sometimes we tend to get bogged down in these things and take ourselves too seriously. Think of the holy person who spends their life sitting on a mountaintop wearing saffron robes and meditating all day and all night. These people may enjoy a rich internal life, but they forego all the wonders, pleasures and rich experiences associated with daily living. Balance between two worlds is called for when Waterbug appears.

Interpretation

When you draw this Glyph, it means that it's time for you to experience life more lightly, and allow yourself to enjoy the sensation of gliding through your experiences.

"Be playful," Waterbug says to us, "Lighten up!" If you find yourself taking life too seriously becoming overly concerned with spiritual matters, or hanging desperately onto outdated beliefs, or convictions that no longer serve you, call on Waterbug magic.

And, if you feel as though you may be losing your desire to play, try gliding over the water instead of sinking into it. The Waterbug is one of Nature's most joyful water sprites. Fey-like, playful and light, Waterbug is able to see and be a part of the profound water world which she needs to survive, but always makes time to play. Be as the Waterbug, and you, too, can glide through life effortlessly. At any time you can invoke Waterbug magic and know the ease and fun that are part of the great joy of living.

Note: if you take yourself too seriously also look to Tricky Boy.

Exercise

Be as the Waterbug. If you can, actually float in a pool or river or lake, or even in your bathtub at home. Feel how light and buoyant your body becomes if you simply let it float naturally. As a hippo, I cannot float, but I can imagine the sensation of floating, so I do that.

Allow your emotional burdens to drop one at a time into the water and sink to the bottom. As you let the last one fall away from you, get out of the water, dry yourself, and notice how much lighter and freer you feel.

If floating on water is impractical, as it is for me, lie on a soft bed or couch, or recline on your sleeping pillows, close your eyes, and *imagine* yourself floating on a large body of water, or a full, lazy, slow moving deep stream or river. Completely relax your limbs, and allow your body to go limp. Drop your burdens, and once they are gone, get up onto your feet, go through the motion of drying yourself off as though you had actually become wet, and notice how light you feel.

WATERFALL

ABUNDANCE IN DIFFERENT FORMS

Description

Waterfall is represented by squiggly lines flowing from the top to the bottom, right to left, as though a waterfall flowing over a cliff.

Origin

Another of the Power Stones, the meaning of the Waterfall Glyph is pure, cascading, noisy, abundance.

In Feng Shui, water is one of the symbols of abundance. Running water, such as that of a table fountain, is prominent in the Prosperity Corner (per Feng Shui—the furthest left corner of your home as you enter through a door), to attract abundance.

Interpretation

Abundance is not necessarily about money. Waterfall is a reminder that love, friendship, family, good health, nourishment, our beautiful natural worlds, and inner peace are all part of abundance. This message of this Glyph to open yourself to the abundance that is your birthright, pouring over you in its many forms other than money or Rendazian Glow Seeds.

Waterfalls generate energy and oxygen. Be intent on capturing the essence of the waterfall, to receive its life giving oxygen. If you are experiencing a lack of abundance in your life try this: if you can, visit an actual waterfall, sit near it and allow yourself to experience the abundance in your life. If you cannot visit an actual waterfall, buy a waterfall painting or print, and hang it in your home where you see it often. Put a moving waterfall screen saver on your computer screen or Crystal Interface. Carry a Waterfall Glyph with you, or wear it around your neck. Be aware of how your circumstances begin to improve as the abundance that the waterfall offers rushes and flows into your life.

When you see an image of a waterfall, whether in reality, in your mindscape, in a photo or movie, you are reminded that that pure abundance is truly yours. You need only recognize it, be grateful for it, and accept it.

If primarily money is at issue, also look to Feoh Cup and Wheatharvest.

Exercise

Several times each day visualize a waterfall. Inhale deeply to receive its magic into every cell of your being. Absorb into all of your cells the waterfall's blessings. With your inner ear, behold the joy of cascading water. With your imagination, experience the constant waterfall of love vibrant health, success, and joy flowing over you and into your life.

WHEATHARVEST

HARVEST, REAPING REWARDS OF LABOR

Description

Wheatharvest is represented by a single stalk of wheat.

Origin

Stalks of wheat are among the oldest symbols on the planet, Earth. Wheat is the foundation for making bread, symbolic of Hu Mankind's source of nourishment. In this context, the single stalk of wheat represents a bountiful harvest.

Interpretation

You have been preparing the ground, carefully sowing your seeds, guarding against weeds and pests, and you have diligently tended your fields. Are you working on an important project? Have you been putting the pieces together of a new business? Have you been striving for months or years to achieve a long-held dream or personal goal? Are you striving to achieve a milestone or goal? Take a moment and think about what that might be.

Wheatharvest is an auspicious sign that it is nearing the time to reap the benefits of your labors. As you begin to collect your rewards, three things are important to remember:

1. Be grateful. Gratitude is the basis for all prosperity. The more gratitude you feel for all that you already have right now in this moment, the more good things you attract,
2. Share your bounty. Good things only continue to come your way as long as you share with others and,
3. Once you've collected your bushels of wheat, it's important to separate the useless chaff from the nourishing grain.

Wheatharvest cautions against mindlessly collapsing into your good fortune, taking great care not to contaminate your bounty by cleaving to those things that do not serve your highest good, such as angry thoughts toward others, hate, doubt, fear and envy. Those are the very things that will cease your continued harvest of blessings. However, if you are generous and keep your heart grateful, and free from chaff, when Wheatharvest appears, you can expect a continued, rich, bountiful harvest. Great fortune and rich nourishment are now made available to you.

Note: Also, look to Waterfall and Feoh Cup.

Exercise

Make a loaf of "Gratitude Bread" with organic flour. Make the bread by hand, or if you do not have hands, or you have paws, claws or feet without opposable thumbs, ask a helper to assist you. Use a basic recipe. As you, or your helper, knead the bread, pray into it. Be thankful for the bountiful harvest that allows you to make and eat your bread.

As the dough rises, visualize the increases in your harvest. As you punch down the bread, with each push into the dough be aware your harvest is so rich that you can actually touch and manipulate your abundance. As the bread bakes and fills the room with its yeasty rich fragrance, think of all the food you have to eat, and all the good things you have in your life. As you slice and taste your bread, notice and appreciate the rich and delicious rewarding flavor resulting from your labors. This bread-making process is gratitude made visible. The more gratitude you have, the richer and more abundant your future harvests.

WHITE LIGHT

FATE, GREAT PURPOSE, "EVERYTHING," GOD'S GLYPH, OR THE GODDESS' GLYPH

Description

White Light is represented by a sun or a star burst.

Origin

White Light is a connection to supreme authority, to enlightenment, radical trust, and to fate. Another Power Stone, this Glyph, heralds the "presence of the infinite," who some refer to as God or the Goddess. Similar to some Rune practitioners' belief in the blank Rune, all that is known is contained within this Glyph.

Interpretation

When White Light comes to you, it may appear as a color such as pink, emerald green, gold, lavender, pale yellow, or as a rainbow. It makes no difference. All colors come from the same light source. Place a crystal in your window, and when the sunlight hits it, you will behold all colors in the spectrum, each a reflection of divine White Light. When you receive this Glyph in a reading, it means that you are intended to fulfill a great mission in this lifetime on this planet, and you are being asked to focus on your purpose with all of your heart. You may be called upon to be a spiritual leader, a teacher, a guide, or someone whose talents result in works that assists people in their spiritual growth, or enriches other people's lives in some way. No matter what path you choose, you are destined to do great things.

White Light tells you to be in this world, but not of it. You still must earn a living, wash the dishes, take care of the children, pay the bills, feed the dog, provide lodging for your house squirrels, but in doing so you are tasked with the responsibility of transmuting each movement, each task, each mundane responsibility into a spiritual experience, a meditation, a prayer for world peace and love, a gratitude mantra.

Even brushing your teeth, or bathing in the river, can become a meditation, a prayer. No matter how much responsibility you have in this day-to-day world, White Light puts you on notice that your purpose is important. Once you have engaged fully with your life's mission, you will make a difference so profound you could help to change the world. By your very existence, you have become an expression of White Light, love made visible. This glyph appears to tell you that you are here to make the world a better place. You are a blessing, and you are blessed in return.

> *NOTE: White Light often also appears to announce a life-changing event. Every time this Glyph appears in the destiny position of my daily reading, I know to expect something huge coming my way.*

Exercise

Imagine yourself surrounded by bright, white light. Ask the Light for guidance. Ask to be shown your purpose. Ask what you can do each day to make a positive difference on your planet, then wait for the answer. It will come to you if you pay close attention, if you listen. Then, acknowledge the answer, and respond accordingly.

Alternately, ask White Light about what huge event may be on the horizon for you. Know that White Light is your fate, and is with you always, surrounding you with love, wisdom, guidance and protection. In this world, you *are* the White Light!

YORUSHI

FORGIVENESS, RELEASING PAST HURT, ACHIEVING INNER PEACE

Description

The symbol of Yorushi is a gate without a door, topped by decorative point reminiscent of an Asian temple, or the Shinto shrine marker, the Torii.

Origin

Yorushi is the Japanese word for "forgiveness." The gate, or "Gate of Forgiveness," allows one to experience the freedom one discovers in forgiving another.

Gates have symbolic meaning going back to ancient times on both of our planets. The torii, a traditional Japanese gate, symbolizes the transition from the mundane or profane to the sacred. The torii marks Shinto shrines, but is also seen in Japanese Buddhist temples.

The Gate of Ishtar is one of eight gates into ancient Babylon, or modern day Iraq. It stands as a symbol of rebirth and reconstruction, and is considered one of the original Eight Wonders of the World. An inscription on the gate attributed to Nebuchadnezzar reads:

"I placed wild bulls and ferocious dragons in the gateways and thus adorned them with luxurious splendour so that people might gaze on them in wonder."

Gates also are part of Tarot (nine of the cards traditionally feature gates), and in the Kabalistic tradition.

Yorusih is the gate one can metaphorically walk through and find (or give) forgiveness.

Interpretation

If Yorushi appears in your life it is because you may need help in letting go of past hurts. You need to forgive yourself and others. Yorushi teaches us that our inability to forgive others and ourselves is why so many of us are in pain. "If you wish to be happy," says Yorushi, "you must first release your hurt through forgiveness." Forgiveness is peace.

If you cannot forgive, you only hurt yourself. Yorushi says to free yourself from pain, you need to recognize this. You still have work to do in this area, because your lack of forgiveness continues to harm you, and is limits your ability to advance on your life's journey. The person or people you refuse to forgive do not suffer because of your inability or refusal to forgive them, but you do.

"My inability to forgive you is like my drinking deadly poison in hopes that you will be the one to die."
— *Anonymous*

"An inability to forgive is like walking through life wearing a backpack filled with rocks"
—*Alan Houston, Hayfork, California*

"The difference between holding on to a hurt or releasing it with forgiveness is like the difference between laying your head

down at night on a pillow filled with thorns or a pillow filled with rose petals."

— *Loren Fischer*

When you are upset over something from the past, or if there is someone in your life, living or deceased, you feel has done something so terrible you can never forgive them, Yorushi opens her gate to you. She invites you to release your past hurts, and walk though into a place of great beauty, emotional freedom, and true peace, but only if you are ready to surrender the pain which you have been clinging to, and only if you are willing to abandon it *before* taking a step through the gate. Yorushi says, "The way to peace is through forgiveness."

Exercise

Sit quietly in a place where you will not be disturbed. Close your eyes, and breathe slowly in and out through your heart. Think of all the hate, anger, and pain from your past. Think of those people who have hurt you so badly that you cannot bear their existence, and you do not feel they deserve your love or forgiveness. Really allow yourself to feel all of that angst, hurt, and bitterness.

Then imagine a stirring in your heart of all that dark hatred, and feel it coming up through your system like toxic bile. Open your maw wide because it is coming out. It is so thick it almost suffocates you. It drops to the floor in front of you. Make it visible, tangible. What does it look like? What does it smell like? Is it alive, or dead? What colors are in all that hate and hurt? What is it's texture? Thick? Watery and thin? Dark brown? Greenish? Is it like a blob of toxic mucous? Does it move in one direction or another? Does it pulsate?

With a big imaginary shovel, scoop every bit up and put it into a big heavy plastic bag, and tie it off at the top. Be sure you seal it well because you do not want any of that horrible stuff to leak out and infect anyone, or pollute the air, the water, and the ground around you. Then drag the bag (how heavy is that bag, anyway?) behind you on a wide, well-worn dirt path, taking care not to snag it on a tree root, or briar bush, or thorn so that it will not tear.

On the path ahead of you, you see Yorushi's gate. It is closed, but as you approach it, it opens. On the other side is a beautiful scene. You have never seen a place so beautiful. What do you see there? Think about what you see. By the time you arrive at Yorushi's gate it is open wide. There is a huge metal dumpster beside the gate. You look down at the bag and say, "Thank you for all that you taught me, but I know longer need or desire to hold onto you." Then hoist that heavy bag of hate and bile over your head, and throw it in the dumpster. Slam shut the trash door and secure it with an enormous steel lock. Remove the key, and throw it so far that it disappears into absolute nothingness.

That garbage cannot get out, or be pulled out ever again. Then walk through Yorushi's gate, close it behind you. Your toxic burden is left in the trash on the other side. What do you feel? What do you see now? What is on the other side of Yorushi's gate? How has your life changed as of this day forward?

ZEPHYR

THE ORATOR, COMMUNICATION THROUGH SPOKEN WORD, LISTENING, HEARING

Description

Zephyr is represented by squiggly lines that mimic breath, expelled as visible lines, like wind might look if we could see wind.

Origin

A zephyr is a soft westerly breeze. It is said that if you listen carefully to the zephyr, sometimes you can hear actual words in the wind.

Wind plays an important role in Hinduism, as the god, Vayu, the source of life breath, or prana, and sustainer of life. In the Upanishads, Vayu is superior to all gods because without breath, a person cannot live.

Wind plays a part in Indigenous Earthly spirituality. Australian aboriginals, for example, see wind as the means to receiving messages from the divine or unseen realms. Indigenous Americans of some tribes honor the wind spirits as harbinger of news. And wind features in both numerology (the number eight), and in Tarot, (the suit of swords).

Of course, the Zodiac features air (wind) signs, too, Libra, Aquarius, and Gemini. People born under these signs are said to love to talk and/or tell stories.

Interpretation

When Zephyr appears, it is time to examine how you communicate, and to work on improving the effectiveness of your communication skills.

Communication is at the center of relationships. Although communication is often non-verbal, and we communicate through a variety of means, Zephyr is all about oral communication, the spoken word, and the skill of reciprocal listening.

Zephyr tells us that listening is the most important part of any conversation. If we talk more than we listen, we cannot hear the breeze rustling the leaves among the trees, we cannot hear the words or thoughts of others, we cannot hear the music of the Universe. If you want to communicate more effectively, or wish to be heard by others, or need to command respect for your knowledge, try listening instead of talking, try silence. Lao Tzu, the author of the Tao Te Ching, tells us "Those who know do not speak, those who do not know, speak."

Zephyr also serves as a reminder to choose your words carefully. Each sound you make, each word you utter, carries with it a unique powerful vibration. Your words go out into the Universe and return like a boomerang, directly back to you gaining in strength and speed as they travel. If you damn or condemn someone, you will bring even stronger damnation and condemnation upon yourself. If you curse another, you will doubly curse yourself. If you use your words to judge another harshly, you will be judged more harshly in return. If you send out words of love, compassion, and kindness, you will attract love, compassion and kindness.

Your words can draw others to you and serve you in getting what you need and want out of life, or your words can create barriers to your prosperity and joy, and can repel others. And, consider the power of the words you speak to yourself. The words you speak to yourself, whether in your thoughts, or out loud, have incredible strength. Never tell yourself that you are stupid, or unattractive, or unable to do something. The more you say these things, the more you become these things. Be loving and kind in how you speak to yourself always.

In a business meeting, often those who use an economy of words and who speak in a low but confident voice, truly listening to others, are those who wield the most power. In a personal relationship, if you wish to make a point, or want to be heard and understood by another, or if you want to convey an important feeling, try lowering your voice instead of raising it. Speak to your loved ones in the soft, warm, comforting voice of Zephyr and notice how quickly your relationships almost magically improve. It is well known that a whisper is far more commanding than a shout.

If you wish to be able to improve your communication skills, or to be able to speak more dynamically and effectively to a group of people, or if you are seeking a way to improve communication one-on-one to enhance your personal relationships, Zephyr can teach you how.

This is the Glyph of the orator. If you are not a public speaker, you may want to join Toastmasters, or a similar group, to hone those skills.

Exercise

The following is a good meditation whenever you notice a slight breeze from the west, or receive the Zephyr Glyph. Sit silently, close your eyes and breathe deeply several times through your muzzle or nose, then focus your entire attention on what you hear. Is a squirrel chattering outside of your window? Is someone's Crystal Interface or blue corn thrashing machine making sound in the distance? Do you hear an elephant passing? Is it raining? Do you hear your own heartbeat? Is a dog barking somewhere? Do you hear Zephyr speaking to you?

Or, try silence. Choose a day in which you commit to silence, not speaking one word throughout the entire day from the moment you awake until you fall asleep in the evening. It seems a contradiction, but the key to great communication is silence. Zephyr tells us that the more we practice being quiet, the more we become in tune with the Universe, and the more powerfully we communicate.

If you want to be heard, practice imitating Zephyr. For an entire day, speak in an intentionally distinctive, clear voice, but be mindful of your volume. Speak softly.

To Conclude Our Time Together

Thank you for choosing The Anam Glyphs. To Hu Mans and Rendazians, and all wise seekers throughout the Universe, Peggy A. Wheeler and I wish you the best life has to offer. May you discover within the Glyphs a useful divination tool, an insightful oracle, a reliable guide to illuminate your path, to provide you with the way to a joyful life experience, and to manifest your heart's desires.

Fare-thee-well, my friends!

Beautimus Potamus

To Know More About Beautimus Potamus

To discover more about Beautimus Potamus and her many adventures, refer to the book, *The Splendid And Extraordinary Life Of Beautimus Potamus*, authored, by Peggy A. Wheeler, available on Earth via Amazon, Barnes & Noble, and all the other usual places. On Rendaz, you may stream this book on your Crystal Interface.

To know more about Peggy A. Wheeler:

Go to www.PeggyAwheeler.com

or amazon.com/author/peggyawheeler